The Mighty Mechanics' Book of SPACE

First published in 2025
by Hungry Tomato Ltd
F15, Old Bakery Studios, Malpas Road, Truro,
Cornwall, TR1 1QH, UK

Thanks to our editor, Julie Tofflemire.

Beetle Books is an imprint
of Hungry Tomato.

A CIP catalog record for this book is available from the British Library.

ISBN 9781835690963

Printed and bound in China

Discover more at
www.hungrytomato.com

Picture Credits
(abbreviations: t = top; b = bottom; m = middle;
l = left; r = right; bg = background)

NASA image library: 2mr; 6-7m; 7mr; 8-9m; 8ml; 10-11m; 10ml; 12-13m; 12bl; 16-17m; 17tr; 18-19m; 19tr; 20-21m; 21tr; 22-23m; 23tr; 27br; 28-29m; 29br; 31tr; 34-35m; 35tr; 36-37m; 37br; 38-39m; 39br; 42br; 44-45m; 45tr; 46-47m; 47br.48-49m; 49tr; 51tr; 53tr; 55br; 58-59m; 60-61m; 61tl; 63tr; 65br; 71tr; 77tr. **Wikipedia**: By Esa https://www.esa.int/ESA_Multimedia/Images/2024/04/Ariane_6_media_kit_cover, CC BY-SA 3.0 igo 32-33m; By NASA - https://secure.flickr.com/photos/nasa2explore/12801808743/in/set-72157629601396498, Public Domain, https://commons.wikimedia.org/w/index.php?curid=31384942 74br; By NASA - https://www.jwst.nasa.gov/content/webbLaunch/whereIsWebb.html, Public Domain, https://commons.wikimedia.org/w/index.php?curid=114125719 72-73m; By NASA This file is in the public domain in the United States because it was solely created by NASA. http://www.cubesatkit.com/docs/press/Pumpkin_CSDWLU_2010-2.pdf, Public Domain, https://commons.wikimedia.org/w/index.php?curid=40365069 74-75m; By NASA/JPL-Caltech - http://www.jpl.nasa.gov/news/news.php?feature=4638 (image link), Public Domain, https://commons.wikimedia.org/w/index.php?curid=46433932 70-71m; By NASA/JPL-Caltech - https://www.nasa.gov/sites/default/files/styles/full_width/public/thumbnails/image/rover_drop.jpg?itok=Szjpa6ka, Public Domain, https://commons.wikimedia.org/w/index.php?curid=100088889 57tr; By NASA/JPL/Corby Waste - http://photojournal.jpl.nasa.gov/catalog/PIA07245 (image link), Public Domain, https://commons.wikimedia.org/w/index.php?curid=31199077 66-67m; By NASA/JPL/Corby Waste - http://photojournal.jpl.nasa.gov/catalog/PIA07244 (image link), Public Domain, https://commons.wikimedia.org/w/index.php?curid=339732 66bl; By National Aeronautics and Space Administration (NASA) · Jet Propulsion Laboratory - Published source: Europa Mission Spacecraft - Artist's Rendering " by the Jet Propulsion Laboratory.Direct source: Image hosted by jpl.nasa.gov., Public Domain, https://commons.wikimedia.org/w/index.php?curid=57036736 76-77m; By National Aeronautics and Space Administration (NASA) / Goddard Space Flight Center (GSFC) / University of Arizona / Lockheed Martin. Image, hosted by cdn.phys.org, Public Domain, https://commons.wikimedia.org/w/index.php?curid=50114199 54-55m; By National Aeronautics and Space Administration (NASA), Applied Physics Laboratory - "PEPSSI Instrument Tastes Pluto's Atmosphere" from the Applied Physics Laboratory New Horizons website., Public Domain, https://commons.wikimedia.org/w/index.php?curid=41340864 68-69m; By Ruffnax (Crew of STS-125) - http://catalog.archives.gov/OpaAPI/media/23486741/content/stillpix/255-sts/STS125/STS125_ESC_JPG/255-STS-s125e011848.jpg, Public Domain, https://commons.wikimedia.org/w/index.php?curid=6826183 62-63m; By SpaceX - https://www.flickr.com/photos/spacexphotos/18610429514/, CC0, https://commons.wikimedia.org/w/index.php?curid=41247908 41br; By SpaceX - This image has been extracted from another file, CC0, https://commons.wikimedia.org/w/index.php?curid=65217917 40-41m.
Shutterstock: 3000ad 64-65m; 3DMI 50-51m; Andrew Rybalko (characters throughout); Andy P 4 (welding machine); Annas_Kurniawan 8-9bg, 38-39bg (sky); AriSys 12-13bg; art_of_sun 24-25bg, 42bg (Earth), 53bg (Earth), 70-71bg; Artem Novosad 27bg (moon); Artsiom P 29ml, 52-53m; Banjong Khanyai 14-15m; BlueRingMedia 54 (asteroids); Den Rozhnovsky 26-27m; Dima Zel 30m, 73tr; DniproDD 10-21bg; fukume 2bl, 56-57m; Jemastock 65bg (planet); johnpluto 58-59bg; jongcreative 46-47bg, 74-75bg; Julia Lazebnaya 6-7bg, 10-11bg, 14-15bg; 22-23bg; KanisornP 54-55bg; KK.KICKIN 1bg (moon), 52-53bg, 72-73bg; klyaksun 48-49bg; lukbar 5 (rocket); MaryDesy 2-3bg, 56-57bg; Mechanik 24-25m, 25tr; MN Studios 62-63bg, 76-77bg; Ms Moloko 79br; muratart 69mr; Nerthuz 1m, 42-43m, 80bg; New Africa 4 (pliers); Oceloti 34-35bg,44-45bg, 50-51bg, 66-67bg, 78-79bg; osk1553 32-33bg; PremiumArt 3-4bg, 30-31bg, 60-61bg, 64-65bg; Rvector 4 (headtorch); sdecoret 15mr; Sensvector 1bg (sky), 42-43 bg; SidraArt 39bg (smoke); Sky_light1000 26-27bg; Torsten Pursche 32-33m; Vector A 40-41bg; Vectorpocket 4-5bg; Vegorus 28-29bg, 36-37bg, 68-69bg; VVadyab Pico 18-19bg; Yindee (characters throughout).

Every effort has been made to trace the copyright holders and we apologize in advance for any unintentional omissions.
We would be pleased to insert the appropriate acknowledgments in any subsequent edition of this publication

Contents

Words that appear in **bold** are explained in the glossary.

The Mighty Mechanics

We are the Mighty Mechanics. Welcome to our workshop! We work on some amazing vehicles and machines. Here are a few of the tools we use to fix them.

Launch Pad

This is where a space journey begins! The launch pad is a strong platform that holds the spacecraft until it lifts off.

A tall tower provides platforms for **fueling,** crew entry, and making repairs.

Flame **trenches** help to move fire and hot gases away from the launch pad.

Space agencies reuse launch pads many times, with checks from mechanics and engineers in between, of course!

At liftoff, a huge amount of water sprays out. This absorbs loud sounds that may damage equipment or hurt crew members.

Crew Access Arm

The Crew Access Arm (CAA) is a walkway to the spacecraft. It can also be used to leave the spacecraft in an emergency!

Astronauts make their way down the Crew Access Arm to board the spacecraft.

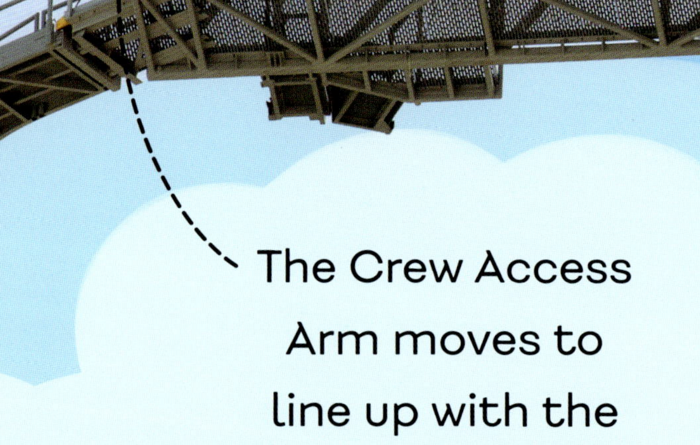

The Crew Access Arm moves to line up with the spacecraft's **hatch**.

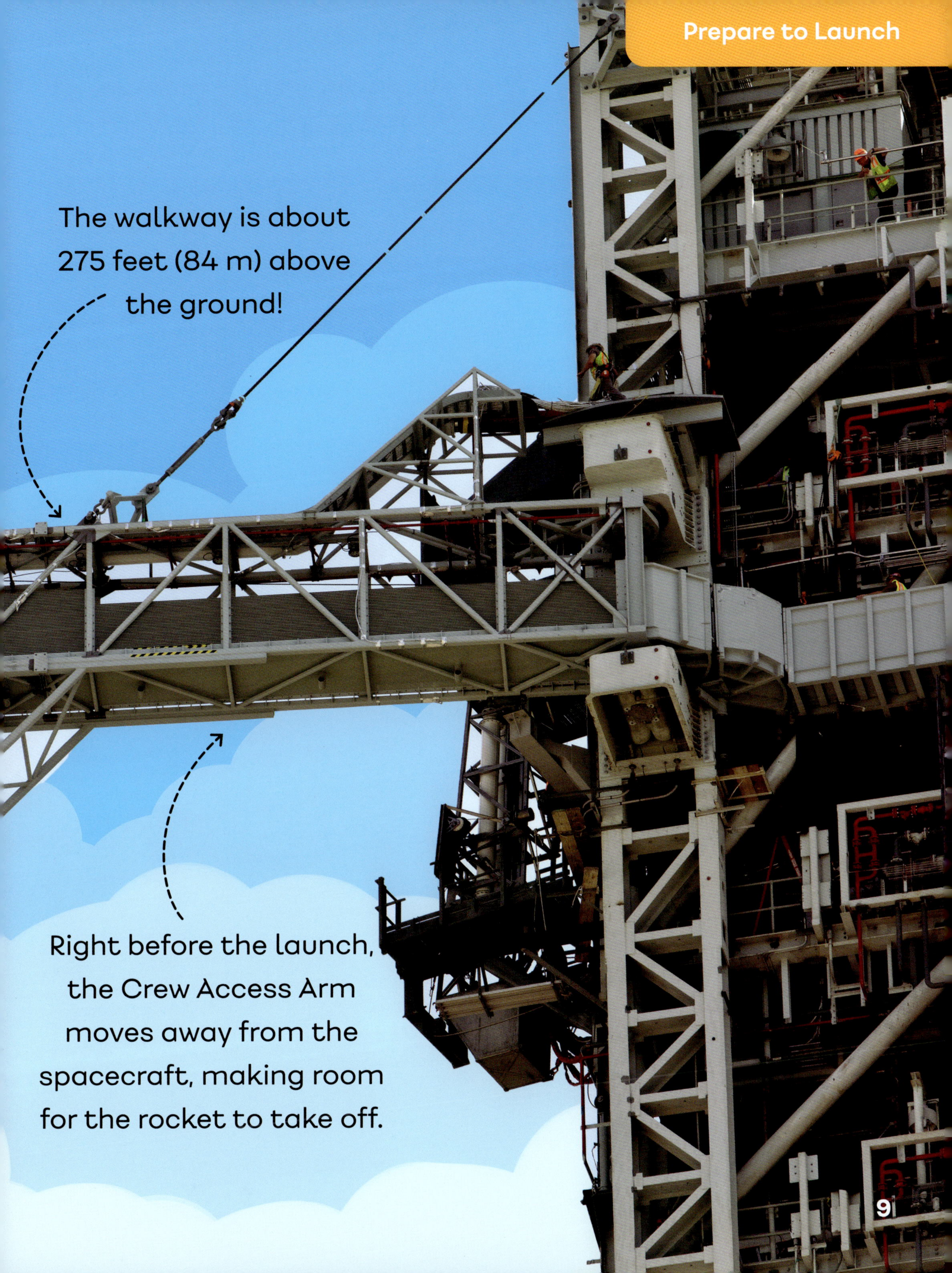

The walkway is about 275 feet (84 m) above the ground!

Right before the launch, the Crew Access Arm moves away from the spacecraft, making room for the rocket to take off.

Crawler-Transporter

The crawler-transporter takes rockets and spacecraft to the launch pad. At NASA's Kennedy Space Center, USA, this trip is 4.2 miles (6.8 km) long.

Instead of wheels, it has eight massive tracks to move the vehicle along.

This huge vehicle is larger than a baseball infield!

The crawler-transporter can carry up to 18 million pounds (8.2 million kg)!

When loaded, its speed is just 1 mile per hour (1.6 km/h). That's slower than most people walk!

Mobile Aerospace Reconnaissance System

The Mobile Aerospace Reconnaissance System, also known as MARS Scientific, provides images from the ground or the sea.
With high-quality data, the safety of space flights will be improved.

The system can be placed on a ship in the Atlantic or Pacific Ocean.

The sections close to protect the equipment.

It can track spacecraft as they launch! It uses a special camera to capture images showing temperature differences.

Even spacecraft moving at more than 3,800 miles per hour (6,100 km/h) can be tracked exactly!

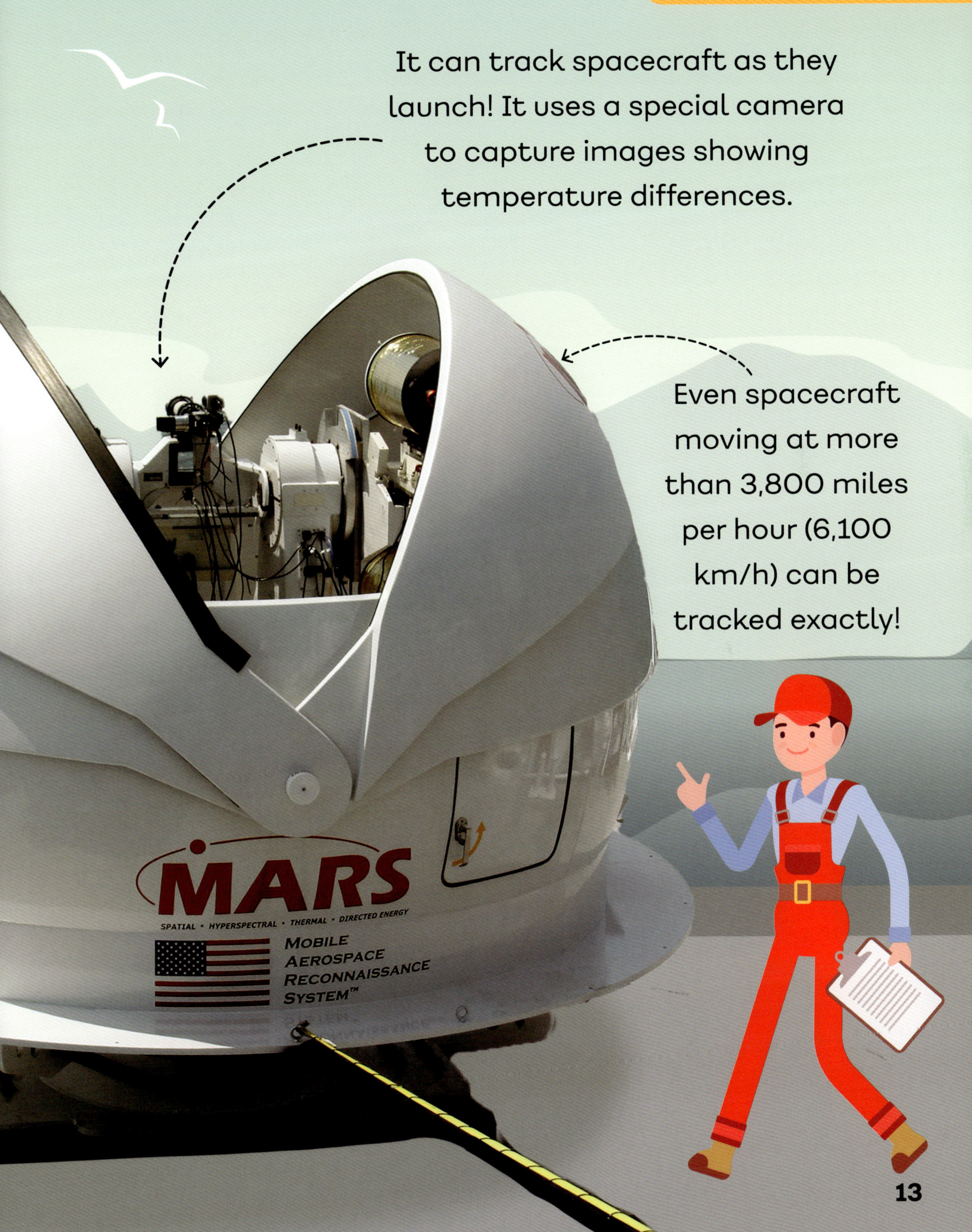

Antenna

We need antennas to send messages into space and receive messages back. They also collect information about what's happening beyond Earth.

By tracking space **debris**, antennas help to protect both crew members and spacecraft.

Ka-Band Objects Observation and Monitoring – also called Ka-BOOM – finds out an object's size, shape, and spin rate.

The antennas of the Ka-BOOM system are 39 feet (12 m) across!

These antennas use **radar** to track objects such as **asteroids** better than **telescopes** that use light.

Crew Transportation Vehicle

After astronauts put on their spacesuits, they need a way to get to the launch pad. The crew transportation vehicle takes them there comfortably and safely.

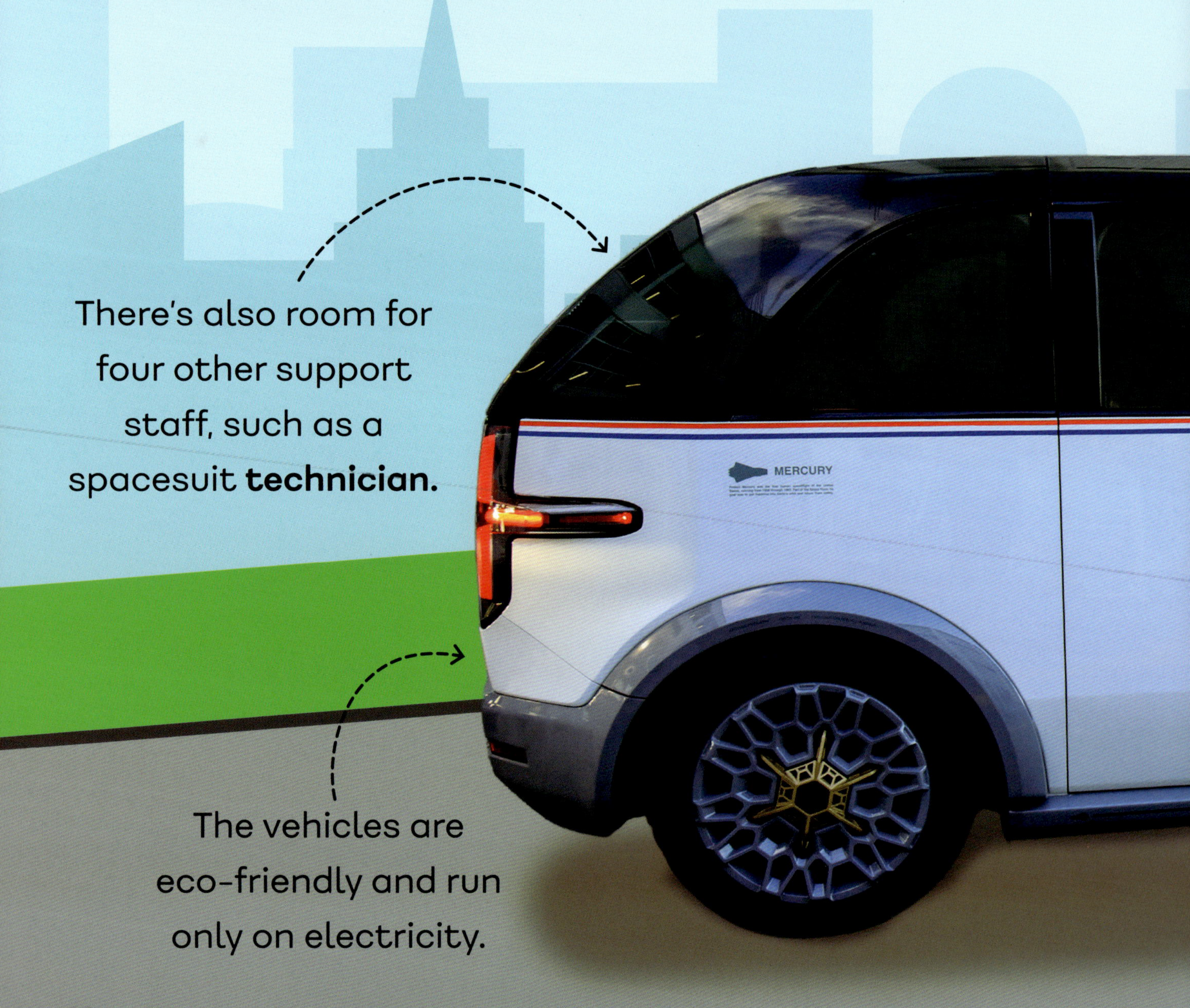

There's also room for four other support staff, such as a spacesuit **technician.**

The vehicles are eco-friendly and run only on electricity.

Spacesuits are big and **bulky!** The vehicle has special seats that can fit four fully suited astronauts.

For Artemis missions, the ride to the launch pad is just 9 miles (14.5 km).

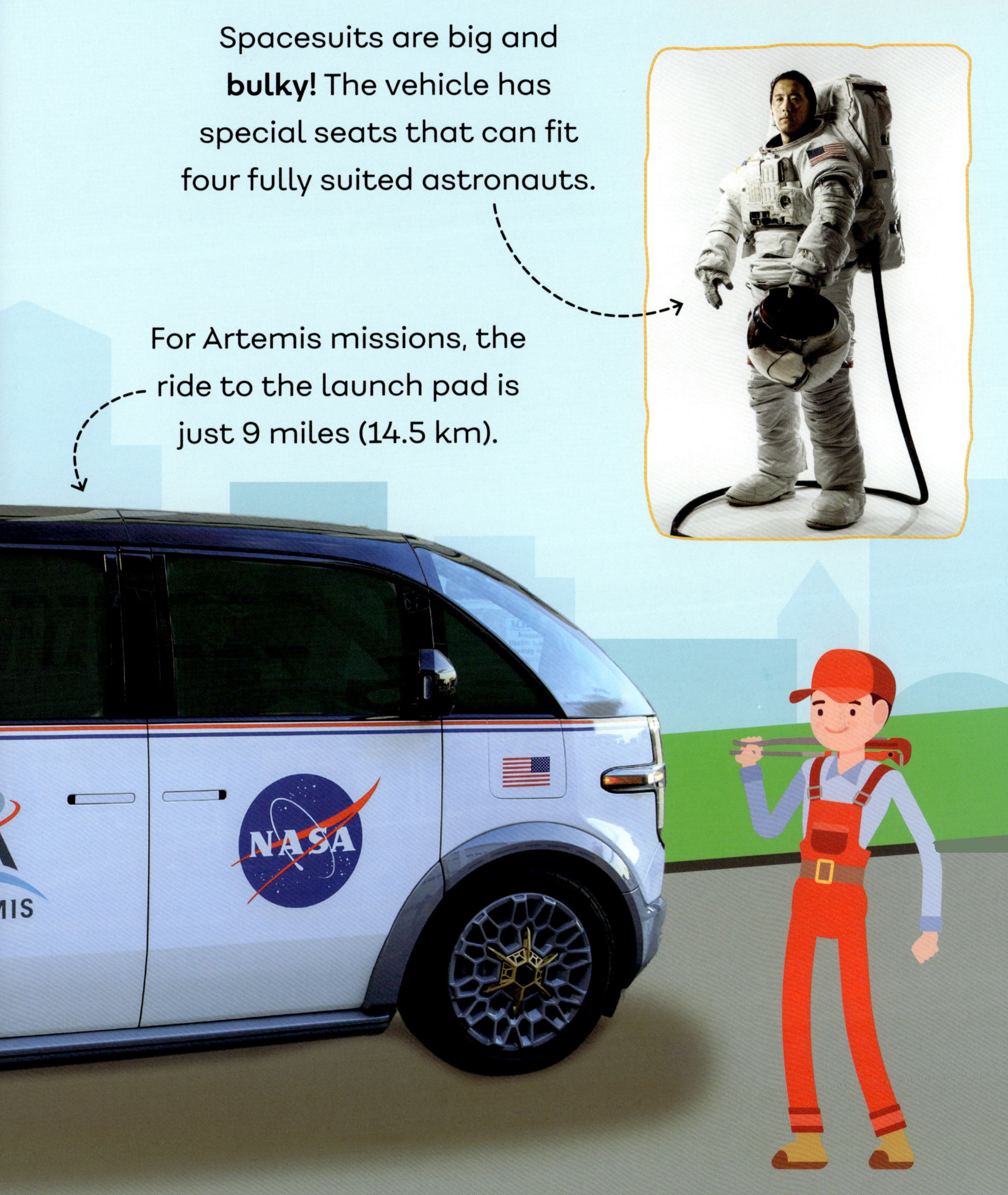

Emergency Egress Vehicle

If something goes wrong with the launch, astronauts need to get away from the launch pad fast! The emergency egress vehicle is there to help.

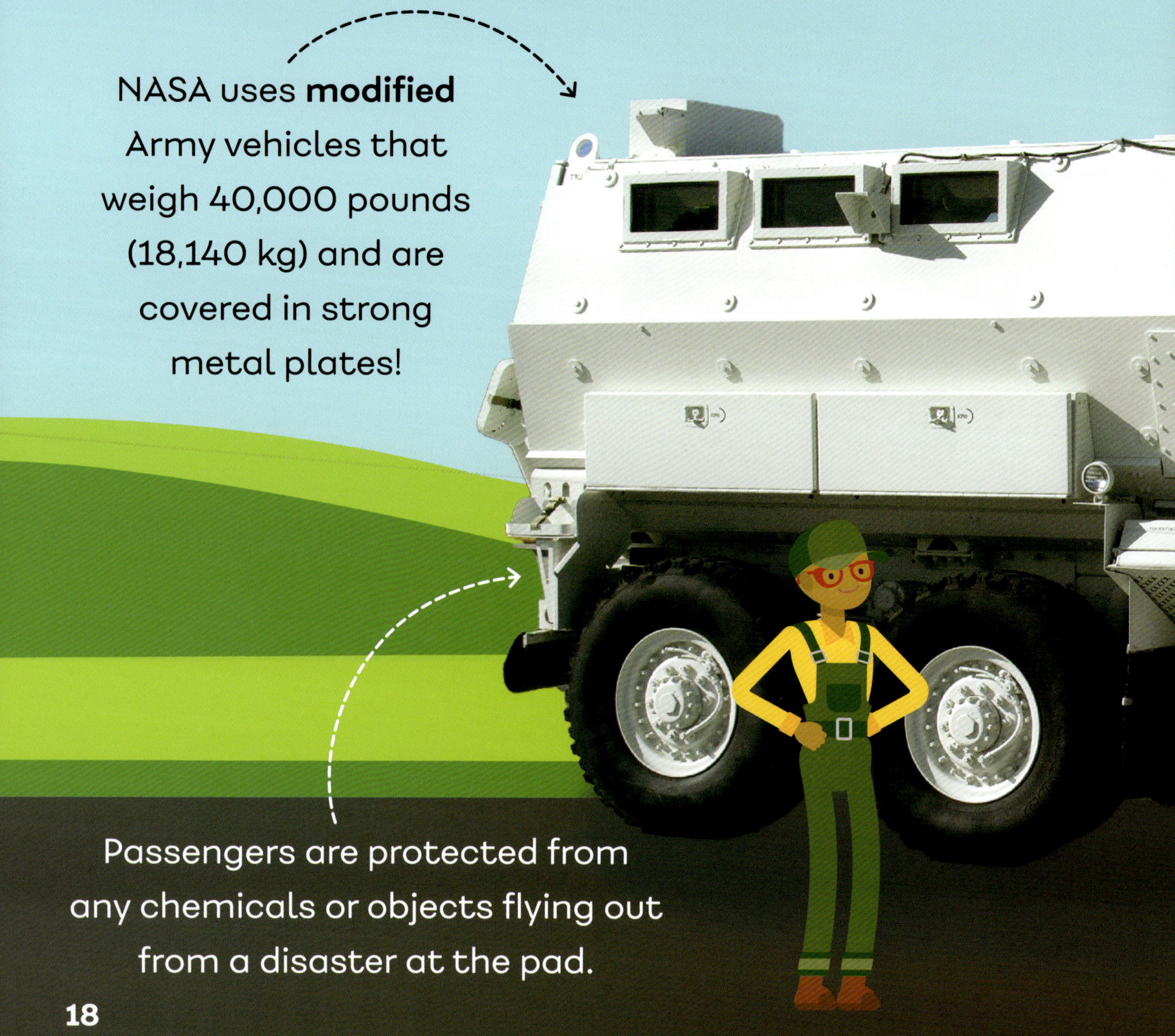

NASA uses **modified** Army vehicles that weigh 40,000 pounds (18,140 kg) and are covered in strong metal plates!

Passengers are protected from any chemicals or objects flying out from a disaster at the pad.

Astronauts slide down a wire in a basket to reach the emergency egress vehicle quickly.

The small windows mean fewer weak points.

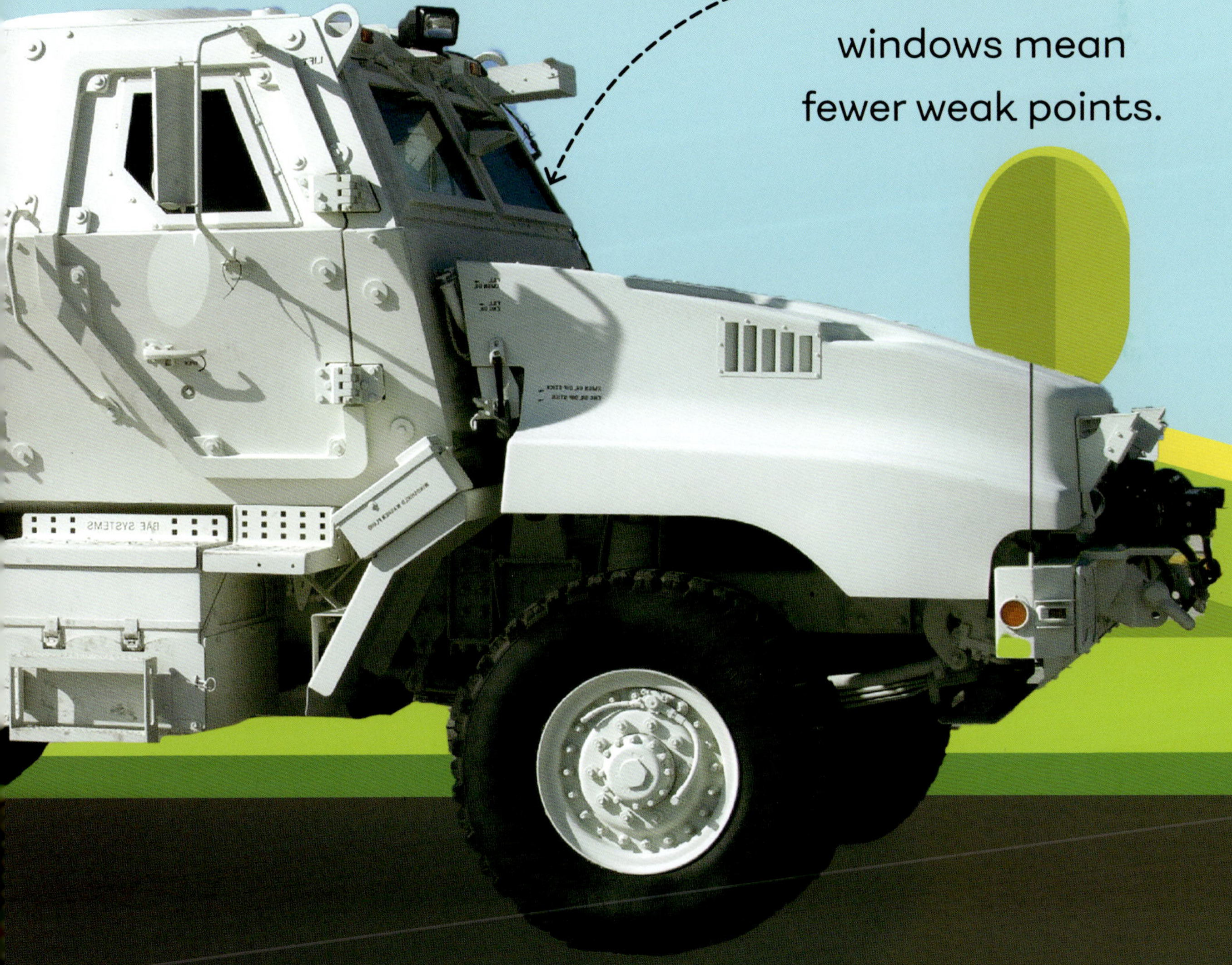

Super Guppy

The Super Guppy is a huge airplane that transports **cargo** that is too big to travel on roads, through tunnels, or under bridges.

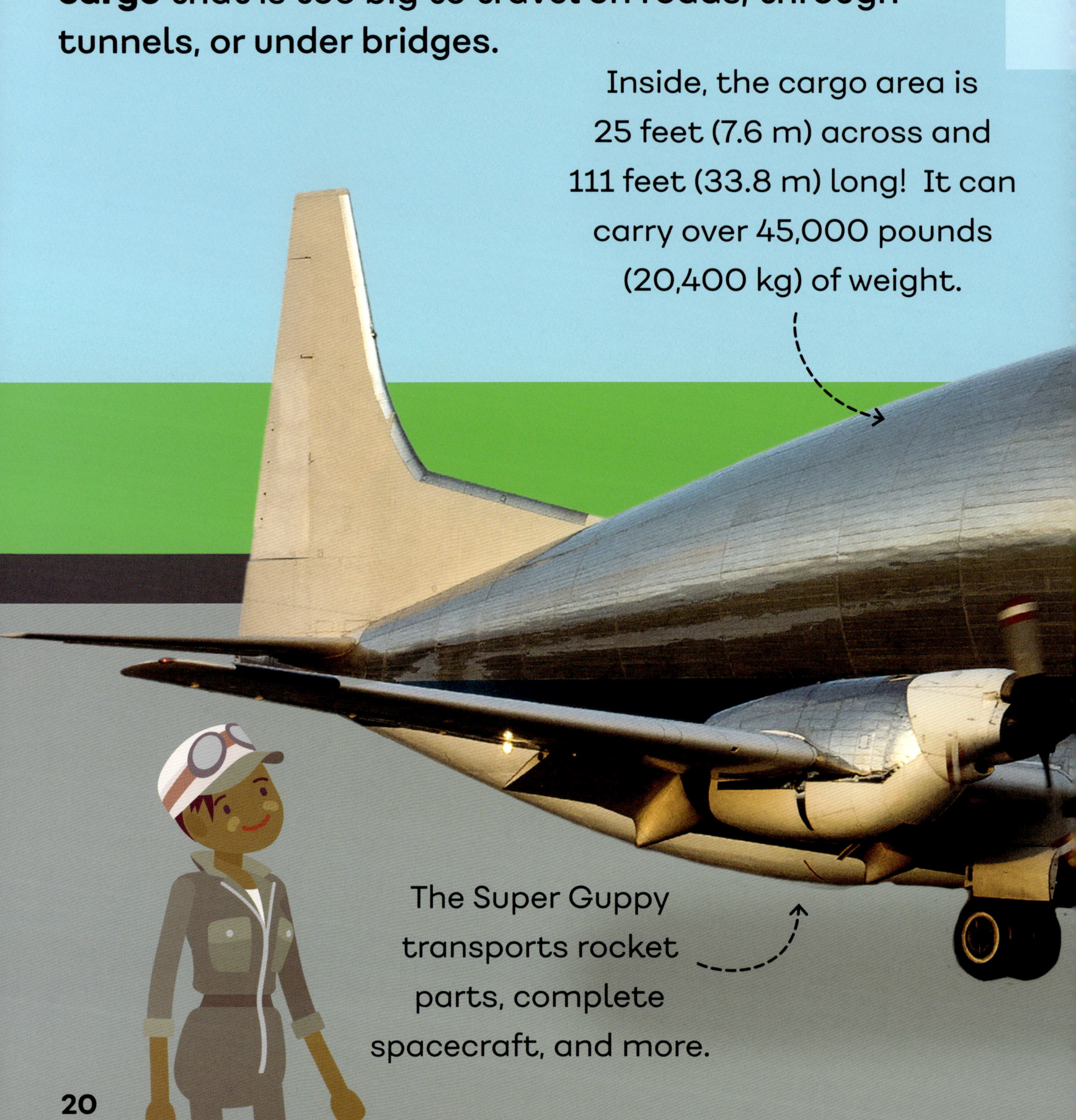

Inside, the cargo area is 25 feet (7.6 m) across and 111 feet (33.8 m) long! It can carry over 45,000 pounds (20,400 kg) of weight.

The Super Guppy transports rocket parts, complete spacecraft, and more.

The nose of the Super Guppy opens like a giant door.

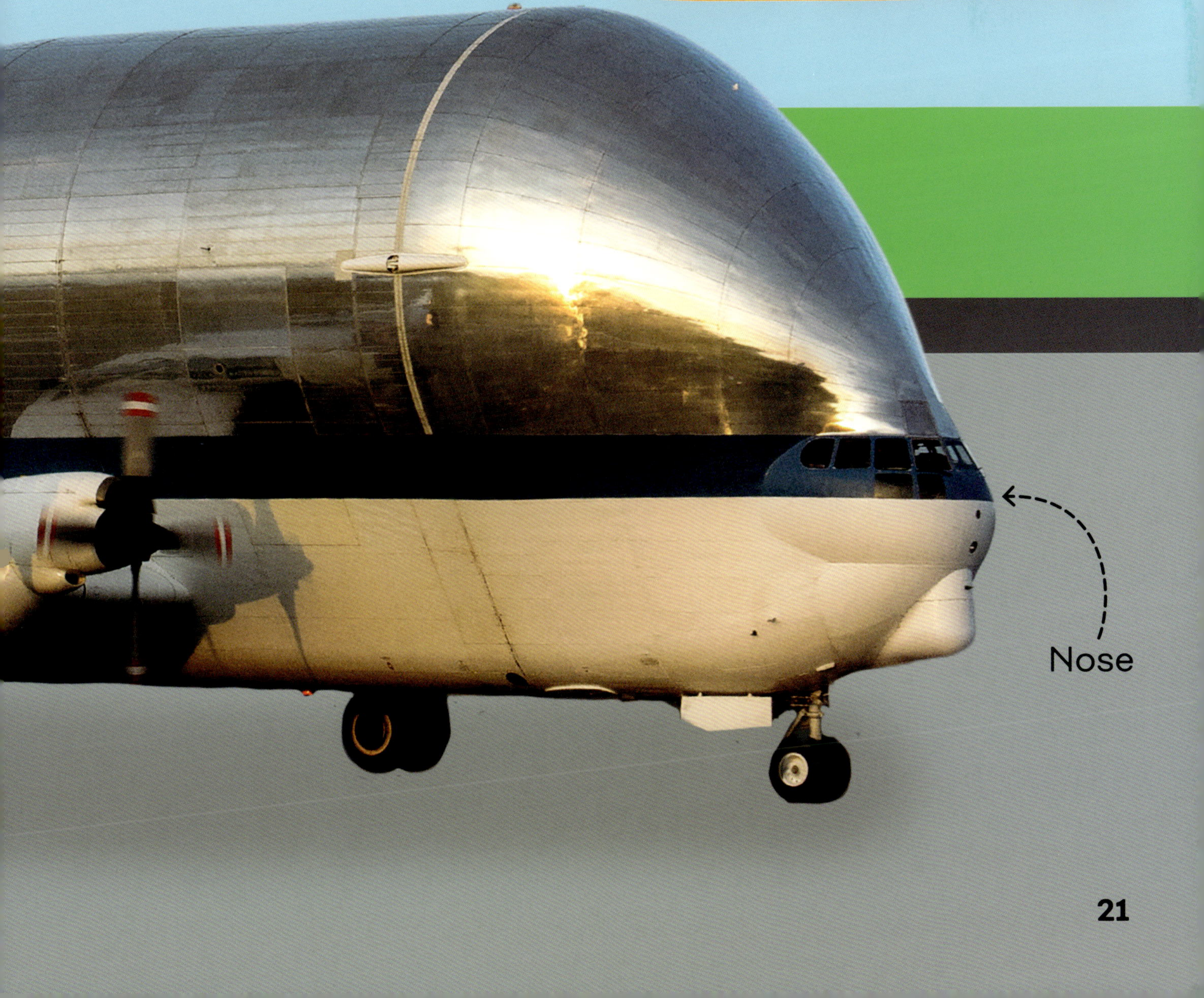

Nose

Ground Test Vehicle

A ground test vehicle is an important step in building a spacecraft. Technicians run tests on the vehicle to learn how the real spacecraft should be built.

Tests check the vehicle's strength and ability to handle pressure. The crew must look for anything that could be dangerous to the crew.

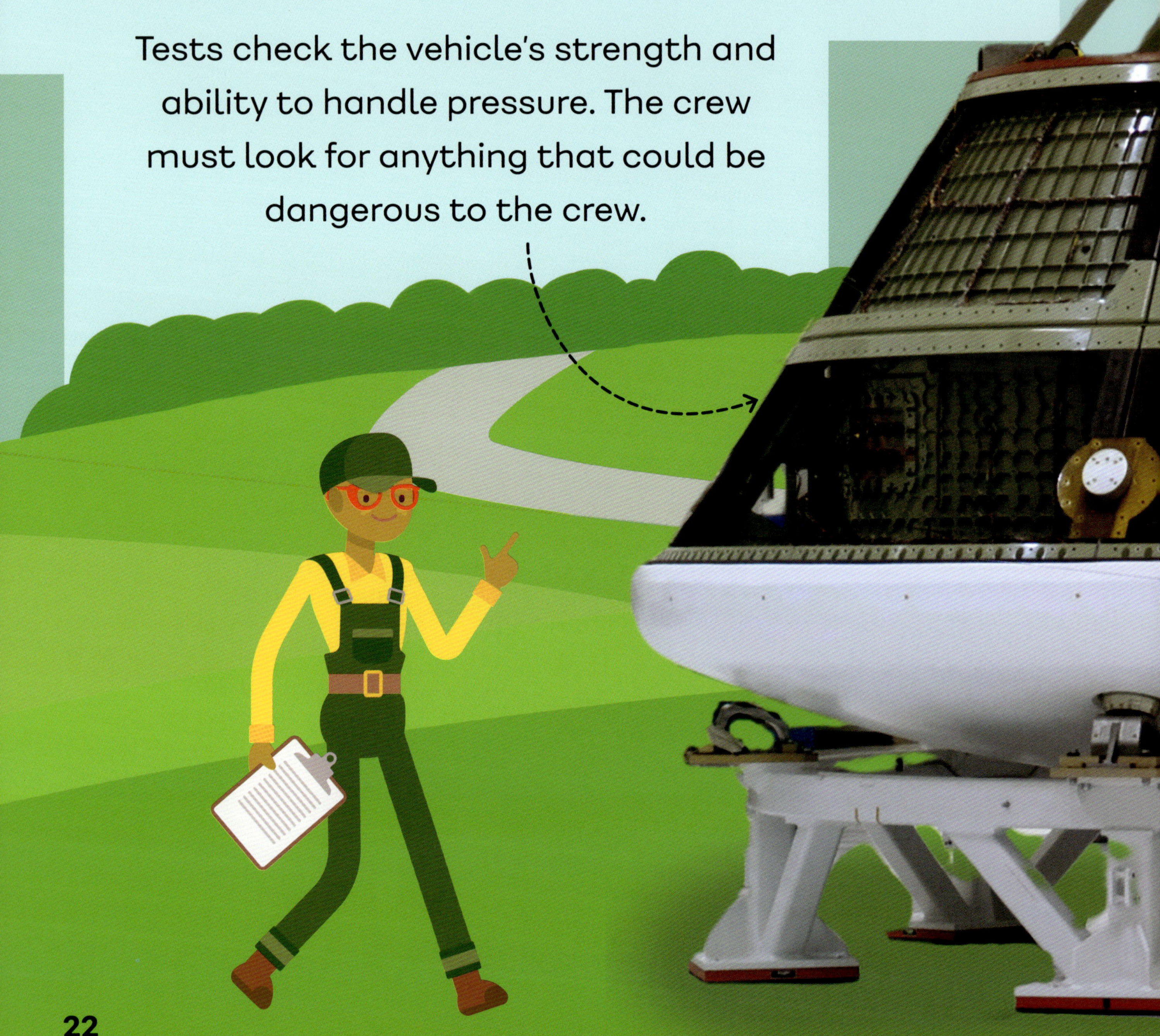

Splashdown tests make sure that a vehicle's **stabilizers** keep it the right way up in the water when it returns to Earth.

If something goes wrong in the tests, there is still time to make changes!

Vostok 1

Vostok 1 was the first spacecraft to carry a human into space! It was launched by the **Soviet Union** in 1961.

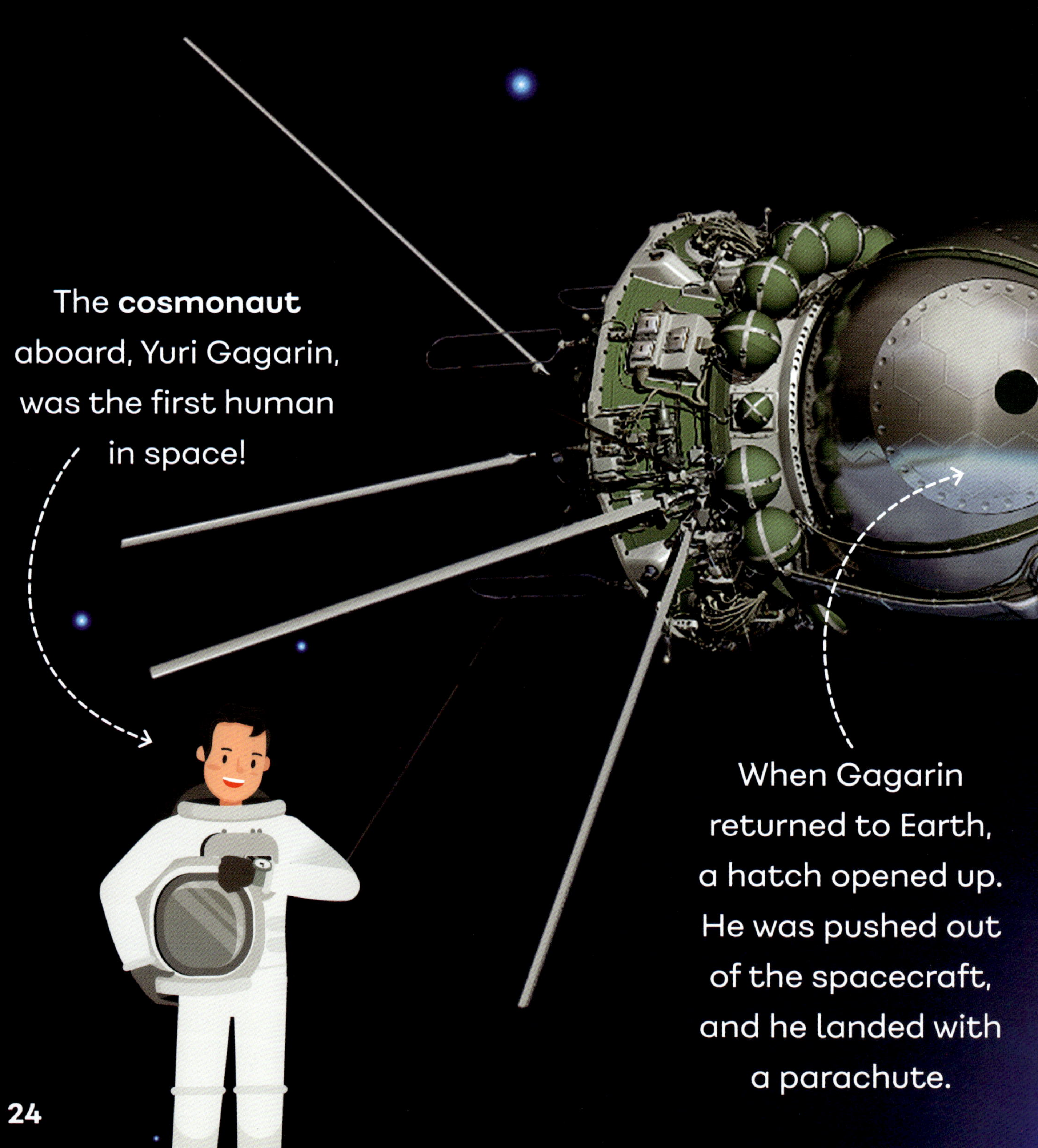

The **cosmonaut** aboard, Yuri Gagarin, was the first human in space!

When Gagarin returned to Earth, a hatch opened up. He was pushed out of the spacecraft, and he landed with a parachute.

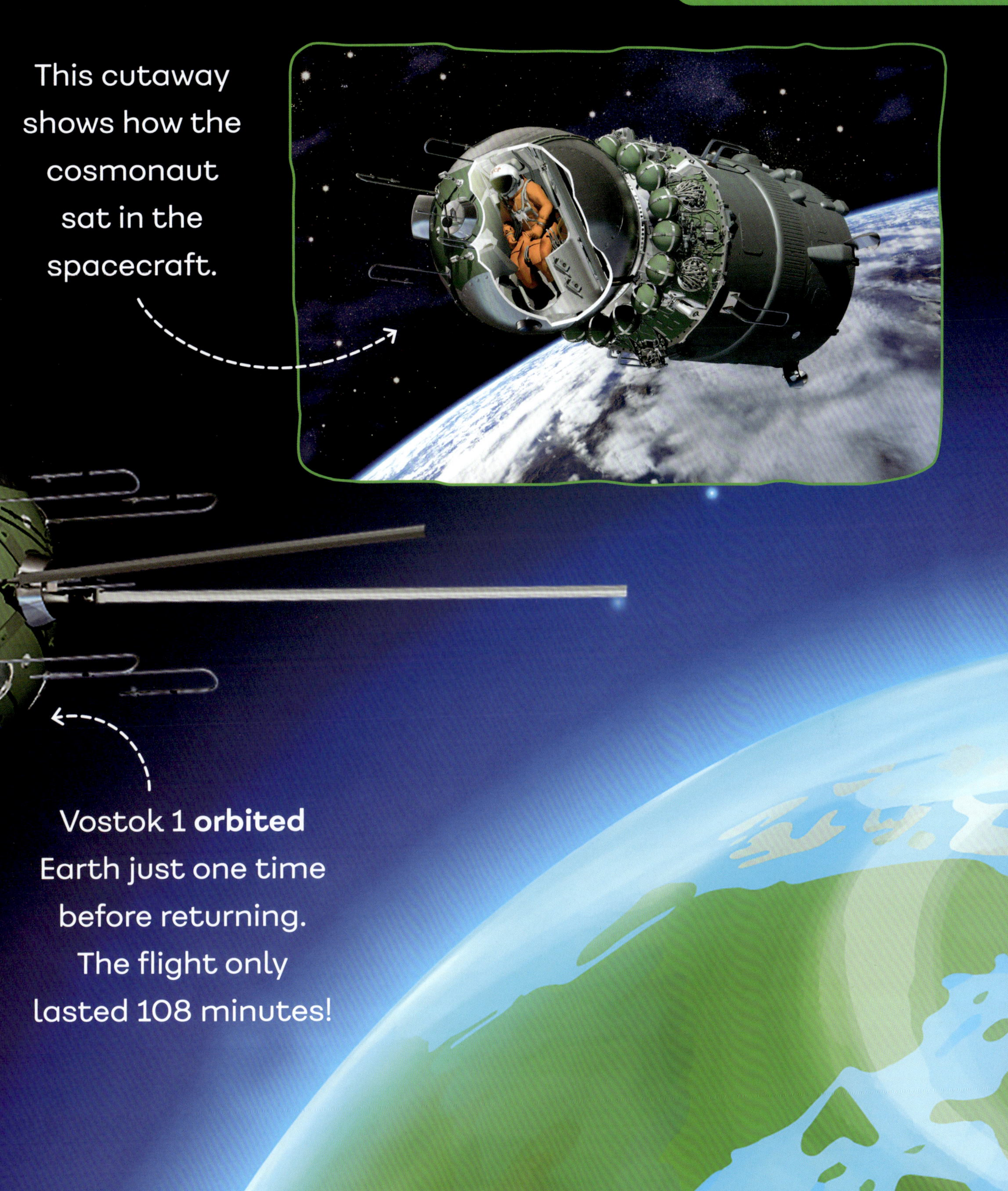

This cutaway shows how the cosmonaut sat in the spacecraft.

Vostok 1 **orbited** Earth just one time before returning. The flight only lasted 108 minutes!

Saturn V

At the time, the Saturn V was the most powerful rocket ever successfully launched. More importantly, it was the rocket that took the first humans to the Moon!

When fully fueled, the Saturn V was about as heavy as 400 elephants!

Like many rockets, the Saturn V's fuel was so cold that ice formed on the outside of the fuel tanks.

Only the **command module** returned to Earth, so pieces of Saturn V rockets are still floating in space!

The Apollo 11 mission that landed people on the Moon for the first time in 1969 was launched using a Saturn V.

Soyuz

Soyuz is the name of both a launcher (rocket) and a spacecraft. These vehicles have been used since 1966 to take people and supplies into space.

The part of the spacecraft where the three crew members travel is about as big as a large van.

Over 1,700 Soyuz launches have already been made, and Soyuz is still going strong!

Powerful engines help the rocket blast into space!

At least one Soyuz is always **docked** at the International Space Station for an emergency trip back to Earth.

Space Shuttle Endeavour

Space Shuttle Endeavour was part of NASA's Space Shuttle Program, which had 30 years of space missions.

The shuttles launched satellites, carried out repairs in space, and helped to build the International Space Station.

To save money, much of Endeavour was built from spare parts!

When returning to Earth, Endeavour landed on a runway like an airplane.

Between 1992 and 2011, Endeavour launched 25 times and flew 122,883,151 miles (197,761,261 km).

Ariane 6

Ariane 6 is the newest rocket used by the European Space Agency (ESA). It carries satellites for science, governments, and companies.

The first launch took place in July 2024. Here, launch equipment for Ariane 6 is getting tested.

Satellites share the ride and are launched in a single flight.

One of Ariane 6's engines can be restarted up to four times.

Ariane 6 can carry light or heavy loads because it has two designs – with two boosters or four boosters.

Orion

The Orion spacecraft can carry up to four people on Artemis missions. It will take humans farther than ever before.

Orion can dock with other spacecraft and even space stations!

The spacecraft's heat shield protects it from temperatures of nearly 5,000 °F (2,760 °C) when returning to Earth!

There are plans for Orion to carry astronauts back to the Moon for the first time in over 50 years!

Dragon

The SpaceX Dragon spacecraft carries both crew members and cargo to space, and it can be used more than once.

SpaceX, a private company, is teaming up with NASA for the launches.

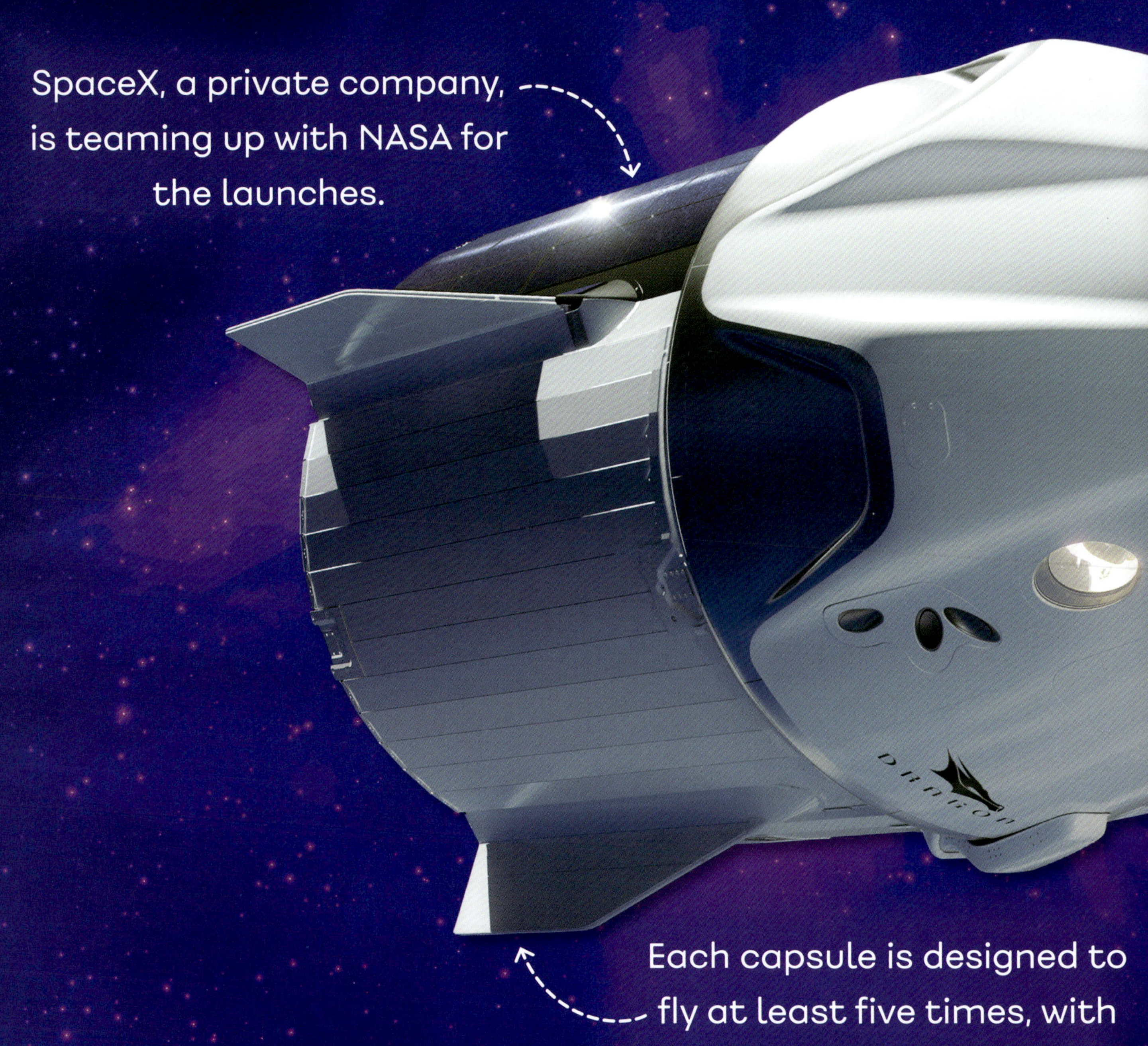

Each capsule is designed to fly at least five times, with repairs between journeys.

The nose of the Dragon opens for docking.

Crew members aboard Dragon wear custom-built helmets with microphones so they can talk to each other.

The spacecraft is designed to carry up to seven crew members.

Electron

Private space company Rocket Lab uses the Electron rocket to launch small satellites into space. The lighter load keeps costs low.

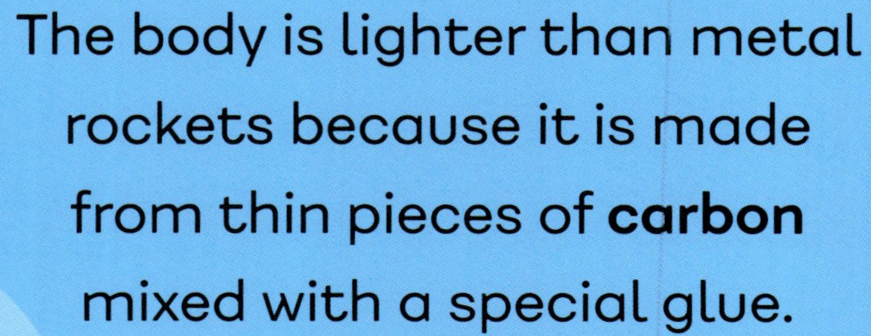

After one launch, while the used booster was falling back to Earth, it was caught by a helicopter (just for a very short time)!

The body is lighter than metal rockets because it is made from thin pieces of **carbon** mixed with a special glue.

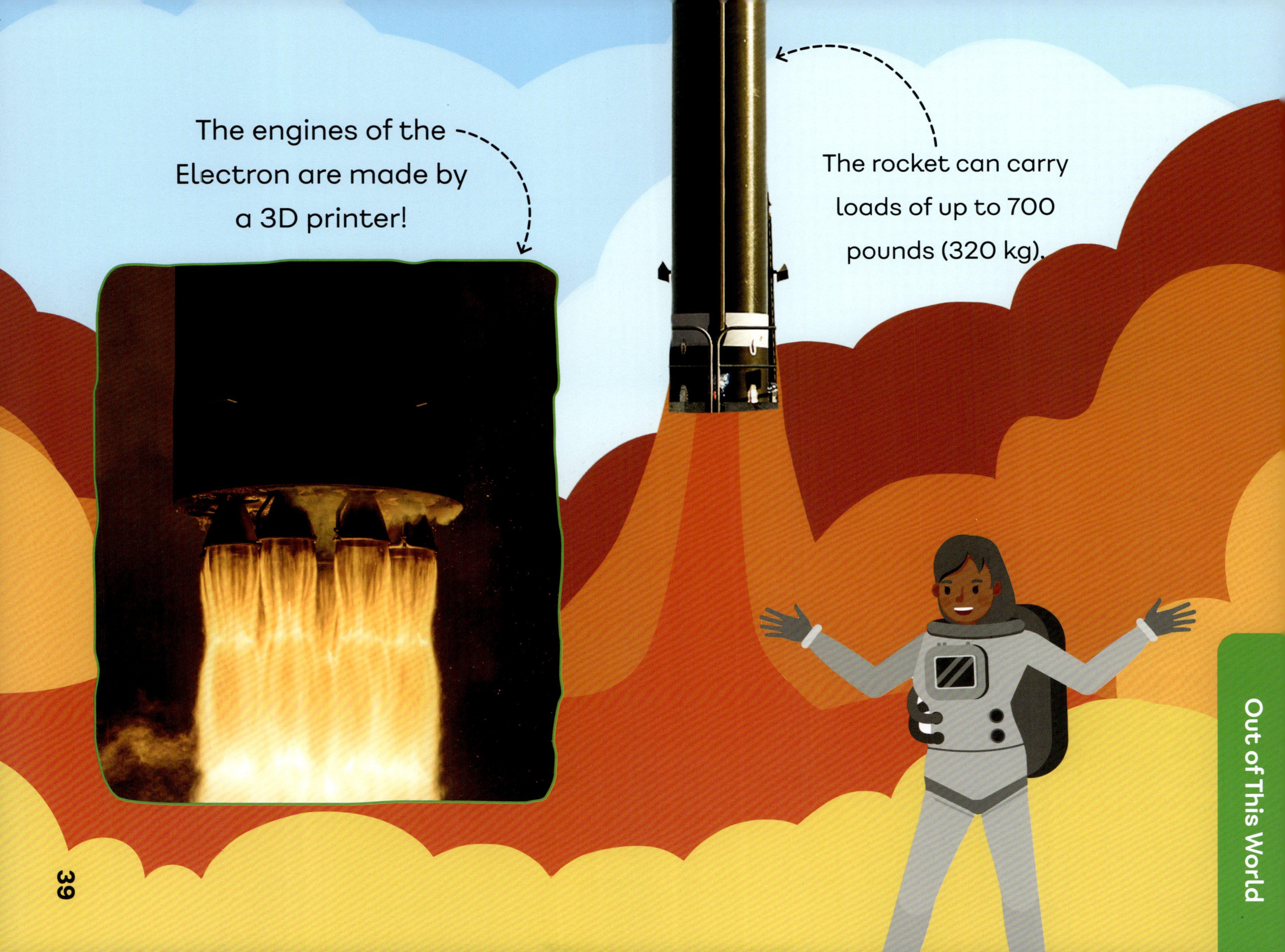
The engines of the Electron are made by a 3D printer!
The rocket can carry loads of up to 700 pounds (320 kg).

Falcon Heavy

Developed by SpaceX, this is one of the world's most powerful rockets! It launches satellites and cargo. It also has reusable parts.

Falcon Heavy is about 230 feet (70 m) in height.

Its power at liftoff is about the same as 18 jumbo jets taking off!

The **payload** is stored at the top. The first test launch sent the company owner's car into space!

SpaceX uses floating platforms to catch and reuse boosters.

Apollo 11 Lunar Module

In 1969, the Apollo 11 lunar module became the first vehicle to land astronauts on the Moon!

It carried Neil Armstrong and Edwin "Buzz" Aldrin, Jr., who were the first people to walk on the Moon.

The module was named Eagle, and when they got to the Moon, Armstrong reported, "The Eagle has landed."

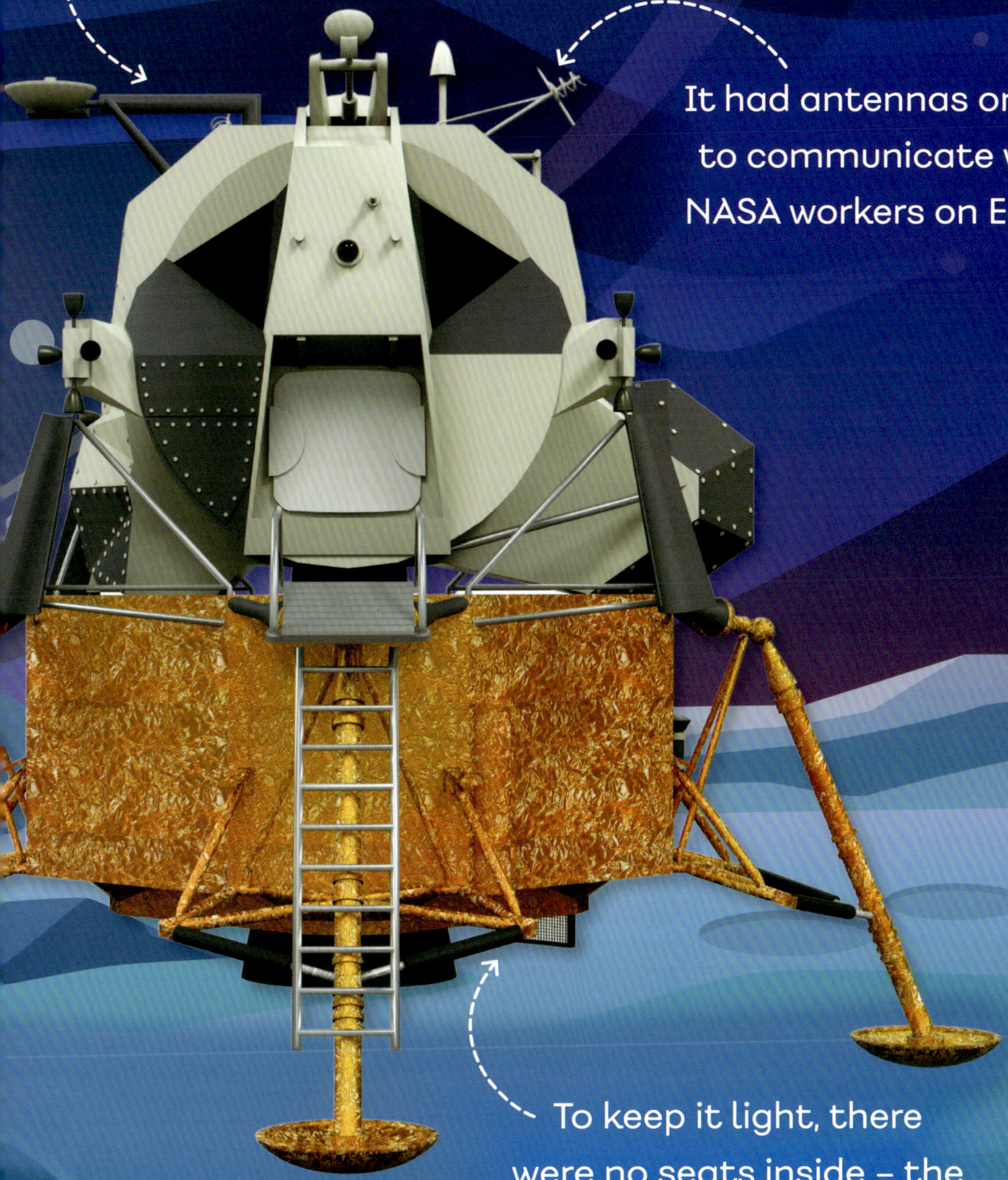

It had antennas on top to communicate with NASA workers on Earth.

To keep it light, there were no seats inside – the astronauts stood up!

Lunar Roving Vehicle

The Lunar Roving Vehicle (LRV) was also called a "moon buggy". Astronauts drove it to explore more of the Moon during Apollo missions in 1971 and 1972.

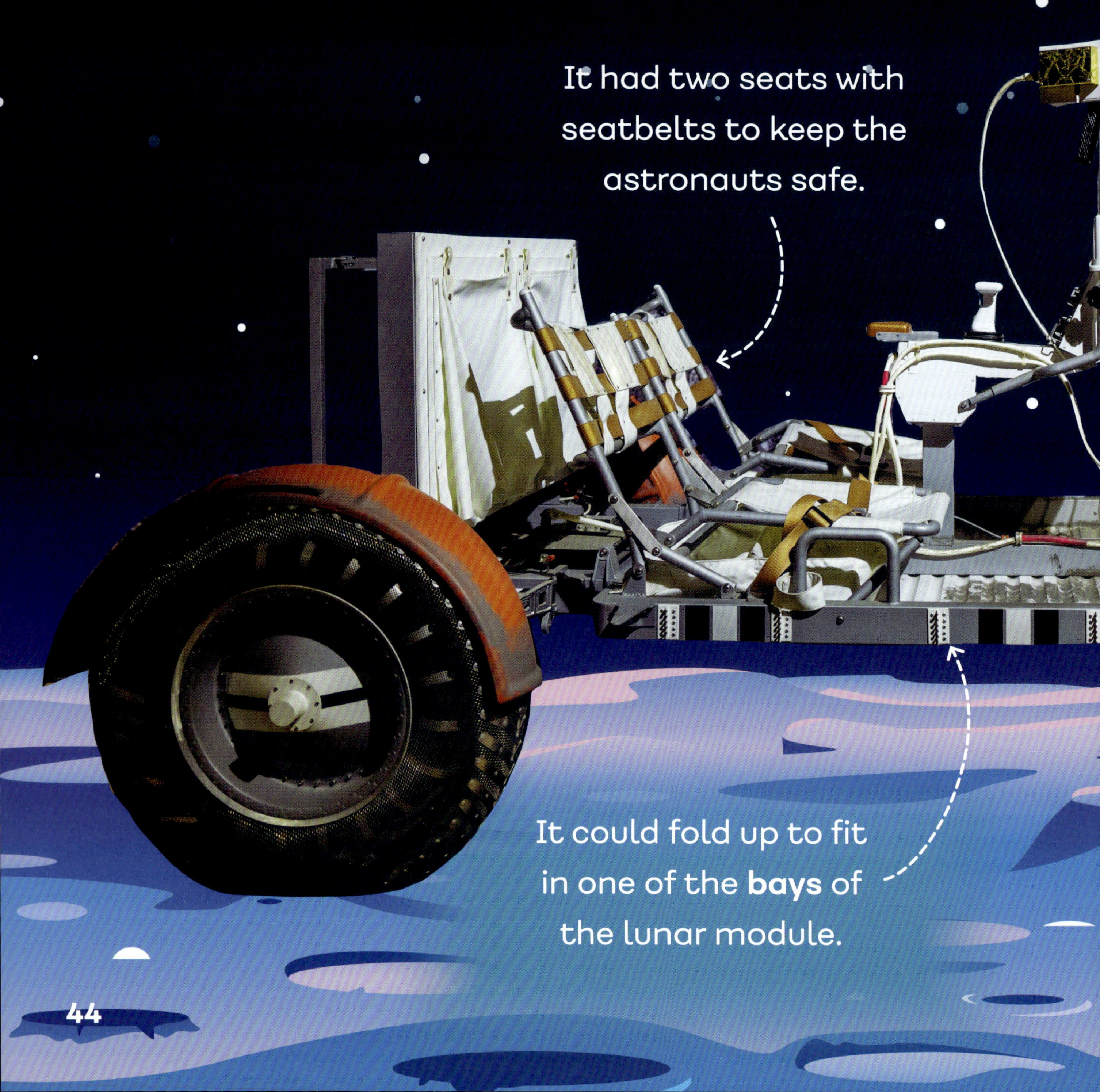

It had two seats with seatbelts to keep the astronauts safe.

It could fold up to fit in one of the **bays** of the lunar module.

Antenna
It had four big wheels to roll over the Moon's bumpy ground.
The vehicle ran on batteries that powered the motor.

Skylab

Skylab was the first American space station. Astronauts lived there to study space, do experiments, and learn how to live in space for a long time!

A Saturn V rocket launched Skylab into space in 1973.

There were three **crewed** missions to Skylab, with crews staying there for 28, 59, and 84 days.

The Orbital Workshop (OWS) was where astronauts worked, ate, and slept.

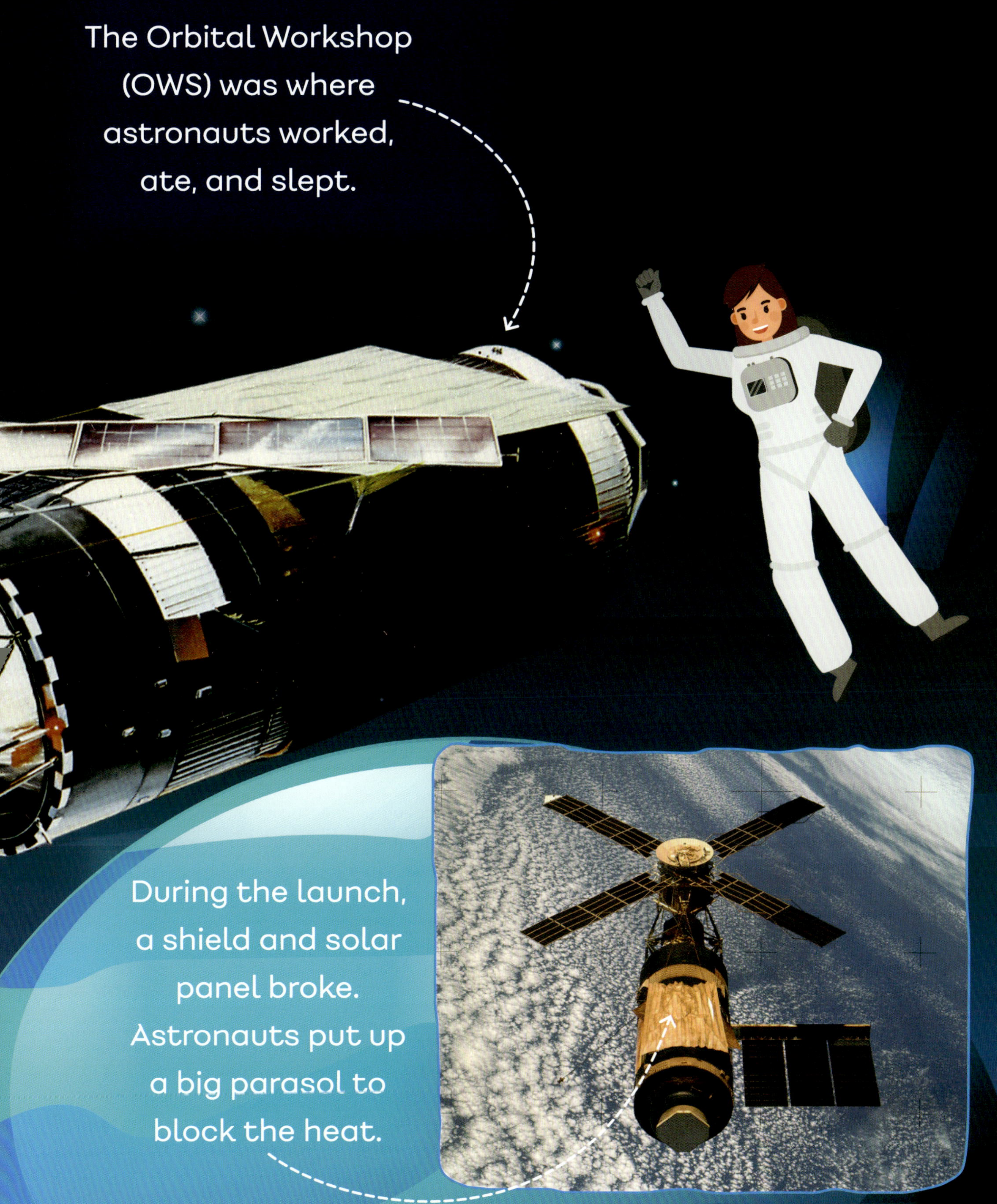

During the launch, a shield and solar panel broke. Astronauts put up a big parasol to block the heat.

Phoenix

Phoenix was a lander that arrived on Mars in 2008. It helped scientists learn about water and life on Mars.

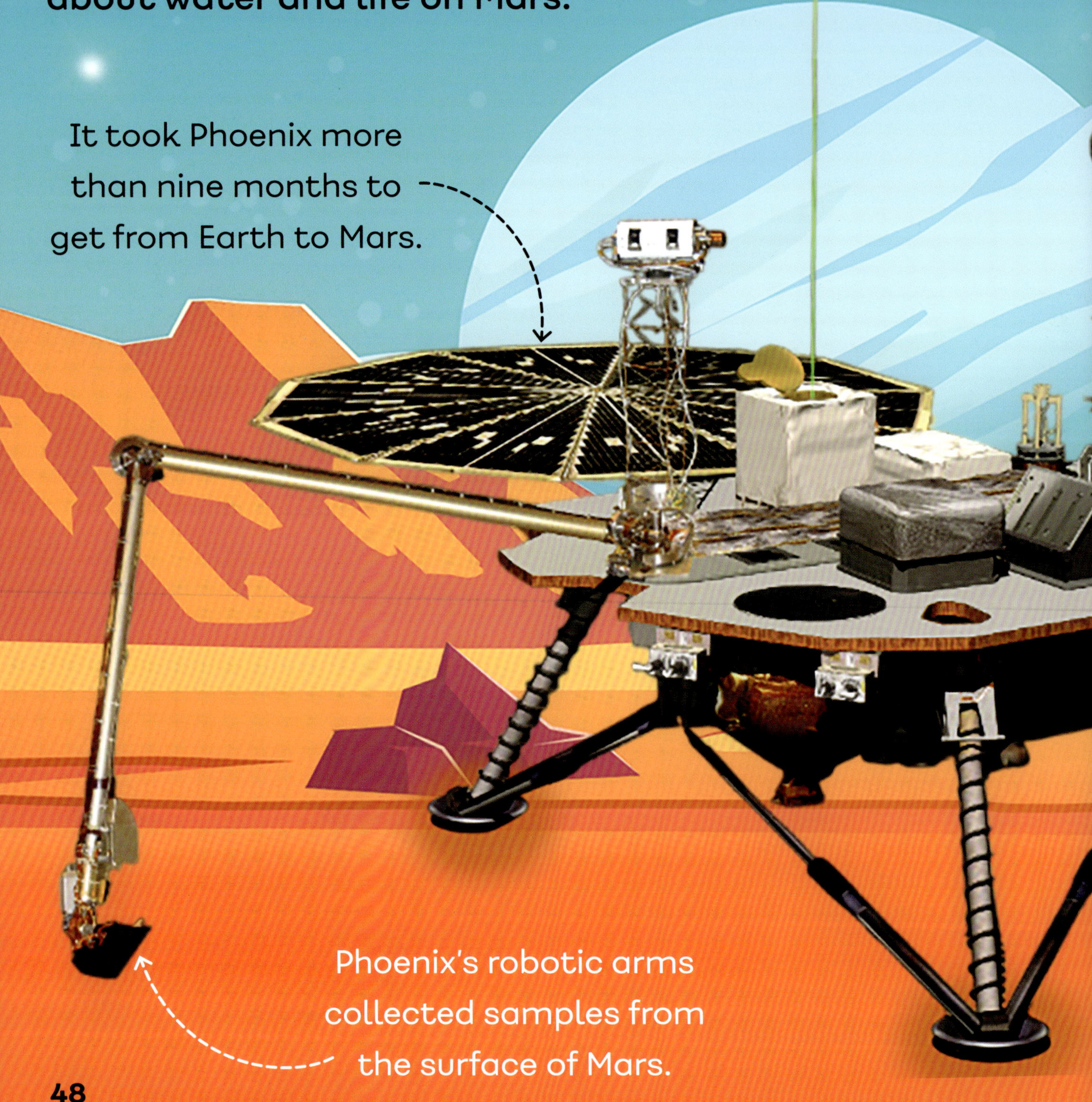

It took Phoenix more than nine months to get from Earth to Mars.

Phoenix's robotic arms collected samples from the surface of Mars.

Phoenix took a picture of itself on Mars – a space selfie!

During its mission, Phoenix found water-ice on Mars!

Sojourner

Sojourner was the first robot rover on Mars! It arrived on the Red Planet in 1997 inside a lander called Pathfinder.

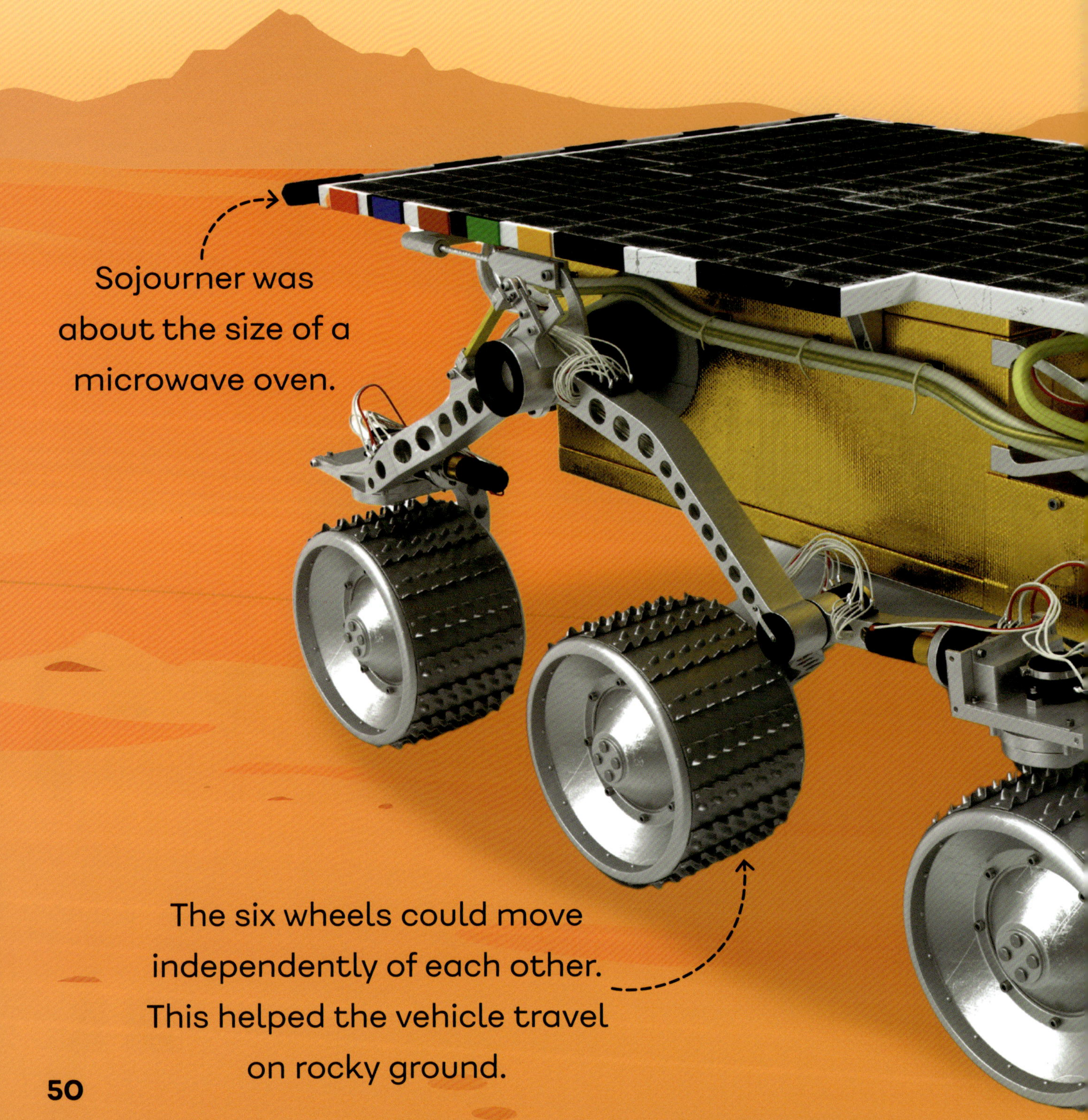

Sojourner was about the size of a microwave oven.

The six wheels could move independently of each other. This helped the vehicle travel on rocky ground.

The rover studied rocks on Mars to find out what they are made of.

Sojourner had cameras to take pictures of rocks on Mars and to avoid **obstacles**.

International Space Station

The International Space Station (ISS) is the largest human-made object in space! It is a giant space lab where astronauts and cosmonauts live and work.

The ISS gets its power from enormous solar panels.

The ISS was built piece by piece in sections. If one part gets old or broken, it can be replaced with a new one.

There is almost no **gravity** inside the ISS, so people and things float around!

About once a month, the ISS fires its engines to give it an extra boost of speed that makes sure it stays in **orbit**!

OSIRIS-REx

OSIRIS-REx is a space probe that flew to an asteroid called Bennu. It grabbed rock pieces there and brought them back to Earth for scientists to study.

The antenna is a big dish used to send and receive data.

The samples were kept safe in the sample capsule.

A long robotic arm reached out, touched the asteroid, and picked up samples from it.

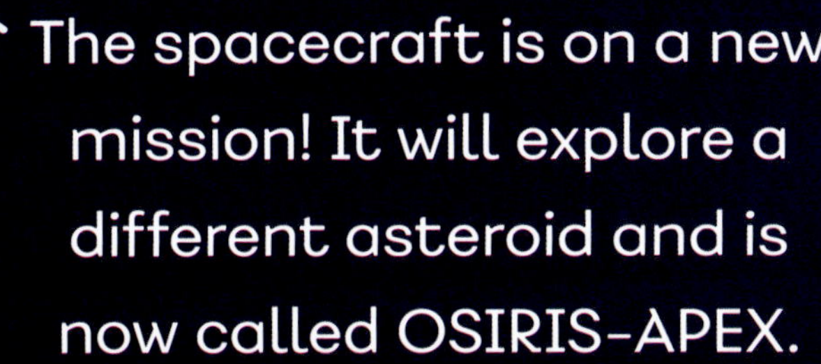

The spacecraft is on a new mission! It will explore a different asteroid and is now called OSIRIS-APEX.

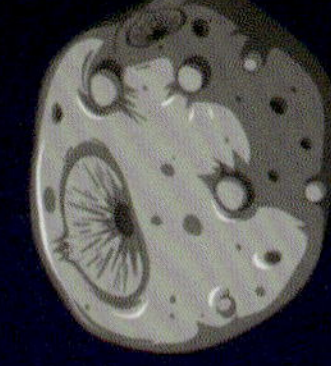

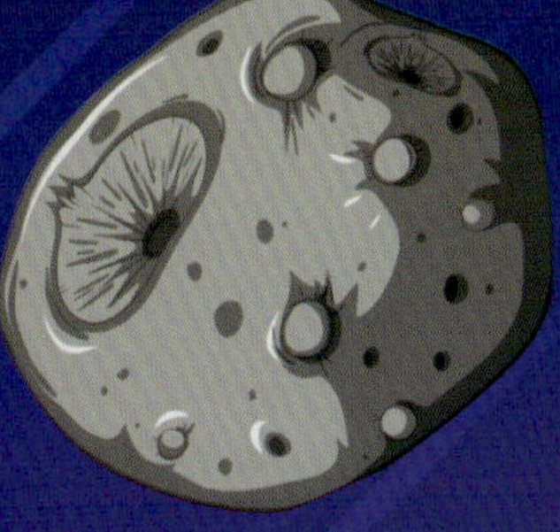

In September 2023, the sample capsule returned to Earth with real pieces of the asteroid inside it!

Perseverance

In February 2021, Perseverance became the fifth rover to land on Mars. It was sent to look for signs of **ancient** life on Mars and collect rocks.

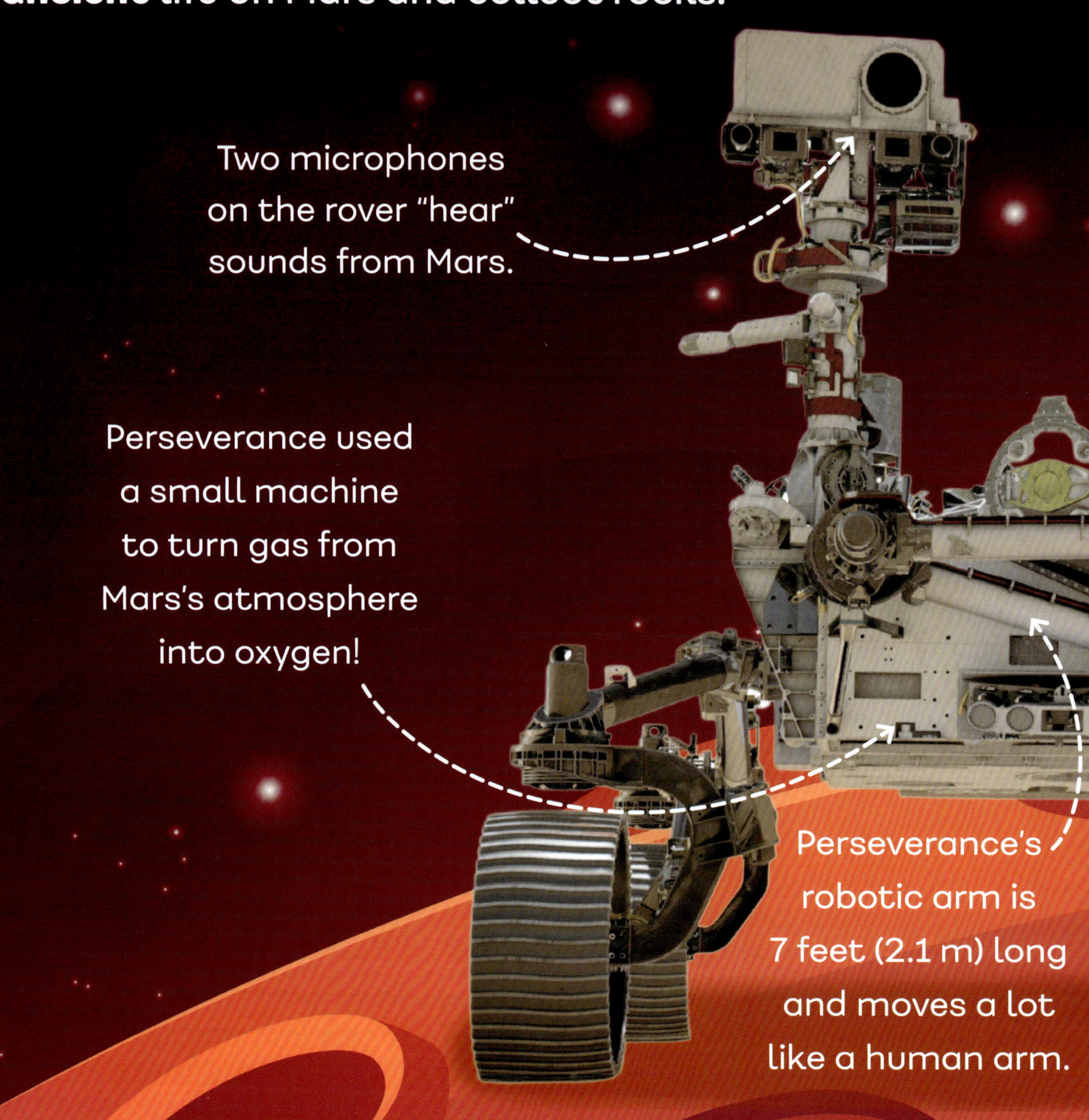

Two microphones on the rover "hear" sounds from Mars.

Perseverance used a small machine to turn gas from Mars's atmosphere into oxygen!

Perseverance's robotic arm is 7 feet (2.1 m) long and moves a lot like a human arm.

To land safely, a "sky crane" from another spacecraft gently lowered Perseverance onto the surface of Mars.

The rover has 23 cameras, including one at the end of its arm.

Ingenuity

Ingenuity was a small helicopter that flew on Mars. It showed that flying on another planet was possible!

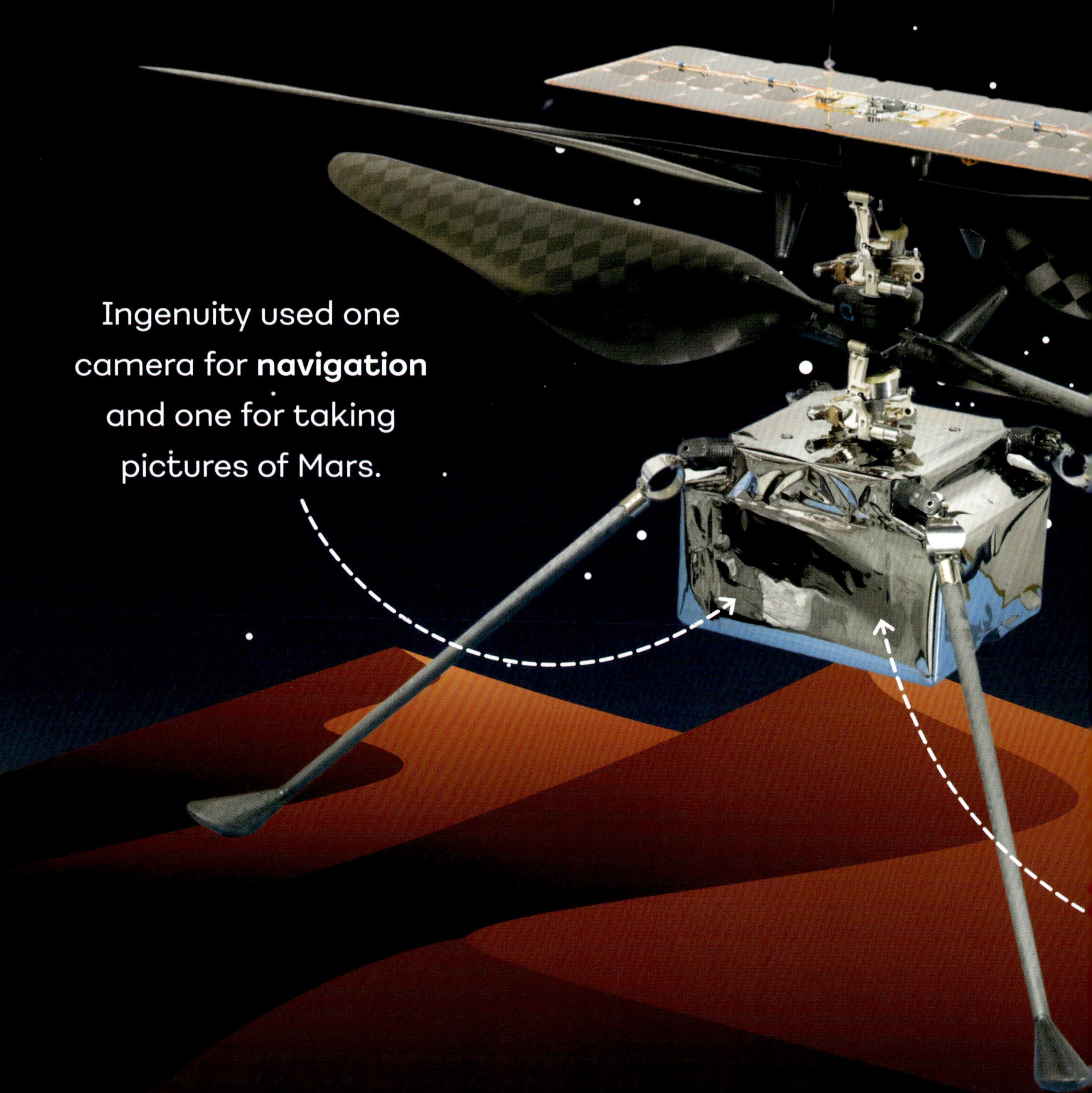

Ingenuity used one camera for **navigation** and one for taking pictures of Mars.

Ingenuity made an amazing 72 flights on Mars before it stopped working!

Its blades spun fast to lift off in the thin air of Mars.

A battery charged by sunlight gave the helicopter the power to fly.

Voyager 1 & Voyager 2

Voyager 1 and Voyager 2 are twin space probes that have been exploring space since 1977. They have traveled beyond our solar system, but they're still sending information to us!

The "bus" holds different scientific **instruments** for the mission.

Voyager 1 and Voyager 2 use a special kind of battery for power. Solar panels wouldn't work because they are so far from the Sun!

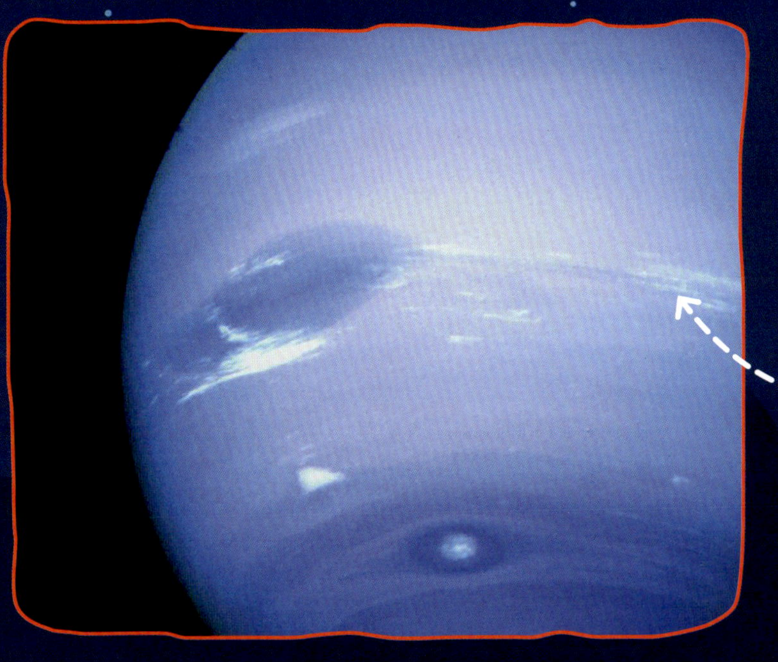

Voyager 2 took amazing pictures of planets, like this one of Neptune.

The huge antenna – which is 12 feet (3.7 m) wide – can send and receive signals all the way from Earth!

Hubble Space Telescope

The Hubble Space Telescope (HST) is a big telescope that was launched in 1990. It orbits Earth and takes pictures of stars, planets, and galaxies to help scientists learn about space.

Hubble sends pictures and information to scientists using antennas.

Its solar panels are huge – they are 40 feet (12.1 m) long!

Hubble has taken many amazing pictures of deep space!

At the front, a special door lets in light, but it can close to protect the inside of the telescope when needed.

Cassini-Huygens

Cassini-Huygens was launched in 1997 and flew for nearly seven years to reach Saturn. The Cassini orbiter studied Saturn and its rings, while the Huygens probe collected information about one of Saturn's moons.

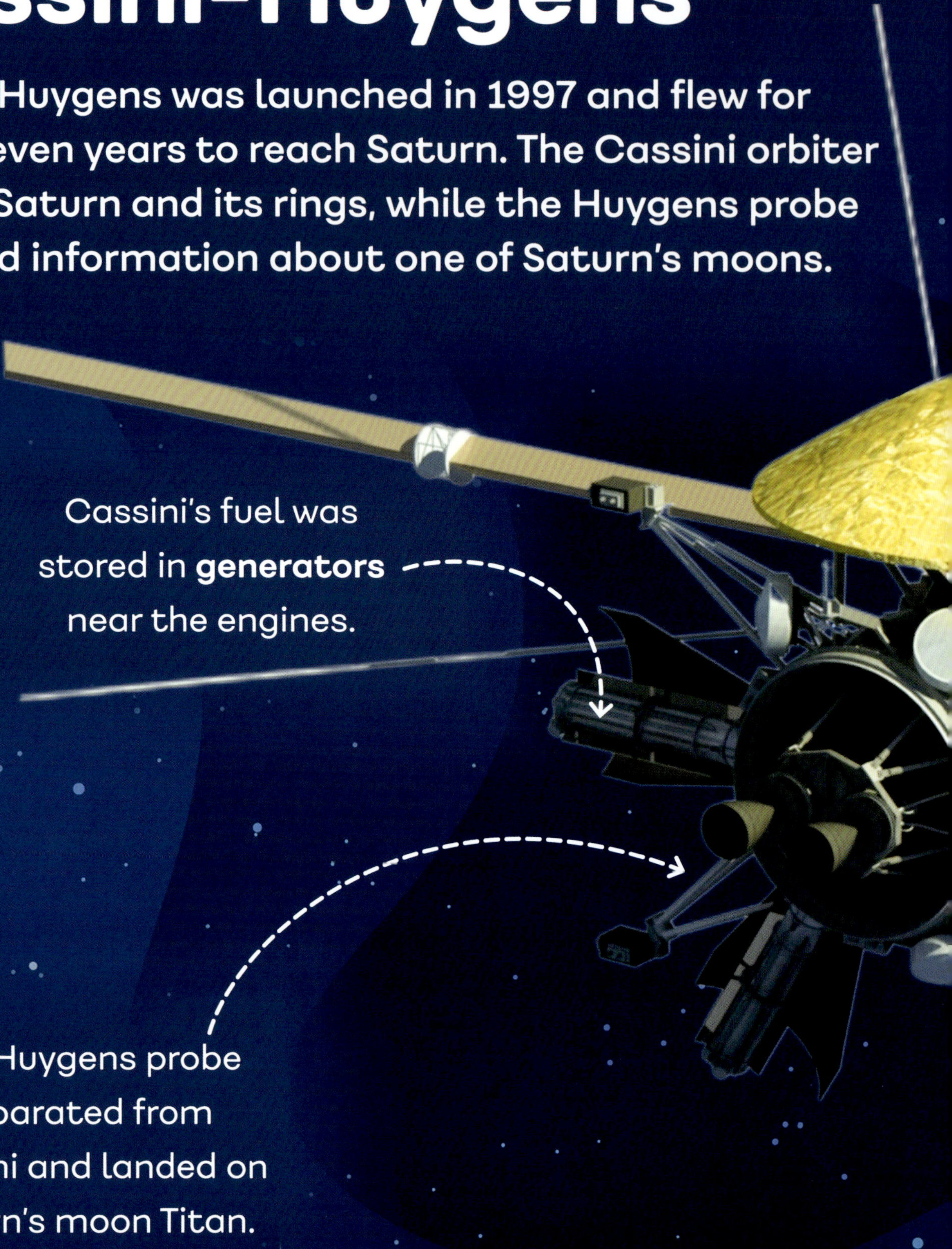

Cassini's fuel was stored in **generators** near the engines.

The Huygens probe separated from Cassini and landed on Saturn's moon Titan.

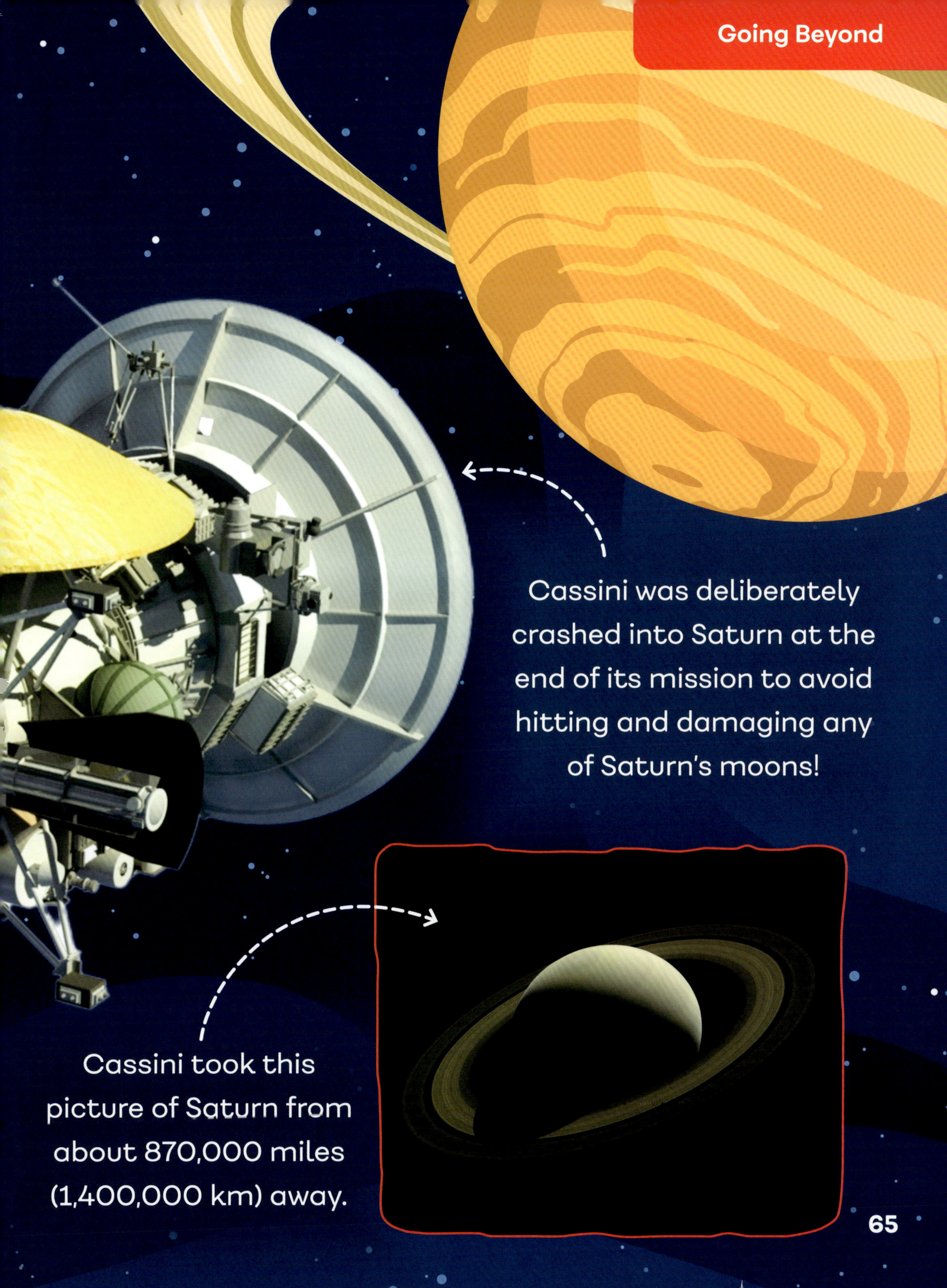

Cassini was deliberately crashed into Saturn at the end of its mission to avoid hitting and damaging any of Saturn's moons!

Cassini took this picture of Saturn from about 870,000 miles (1,400,000 km) away.

Mars Reconnaissance Orbiter

The Mars Reconnaissance Orbiter (MRO) orbits Mars and takes pictures. It is searching for information about the history of water on Mars.

The Shallow Radar, also called SHARAD, hunts for liquid under Mars' surface.

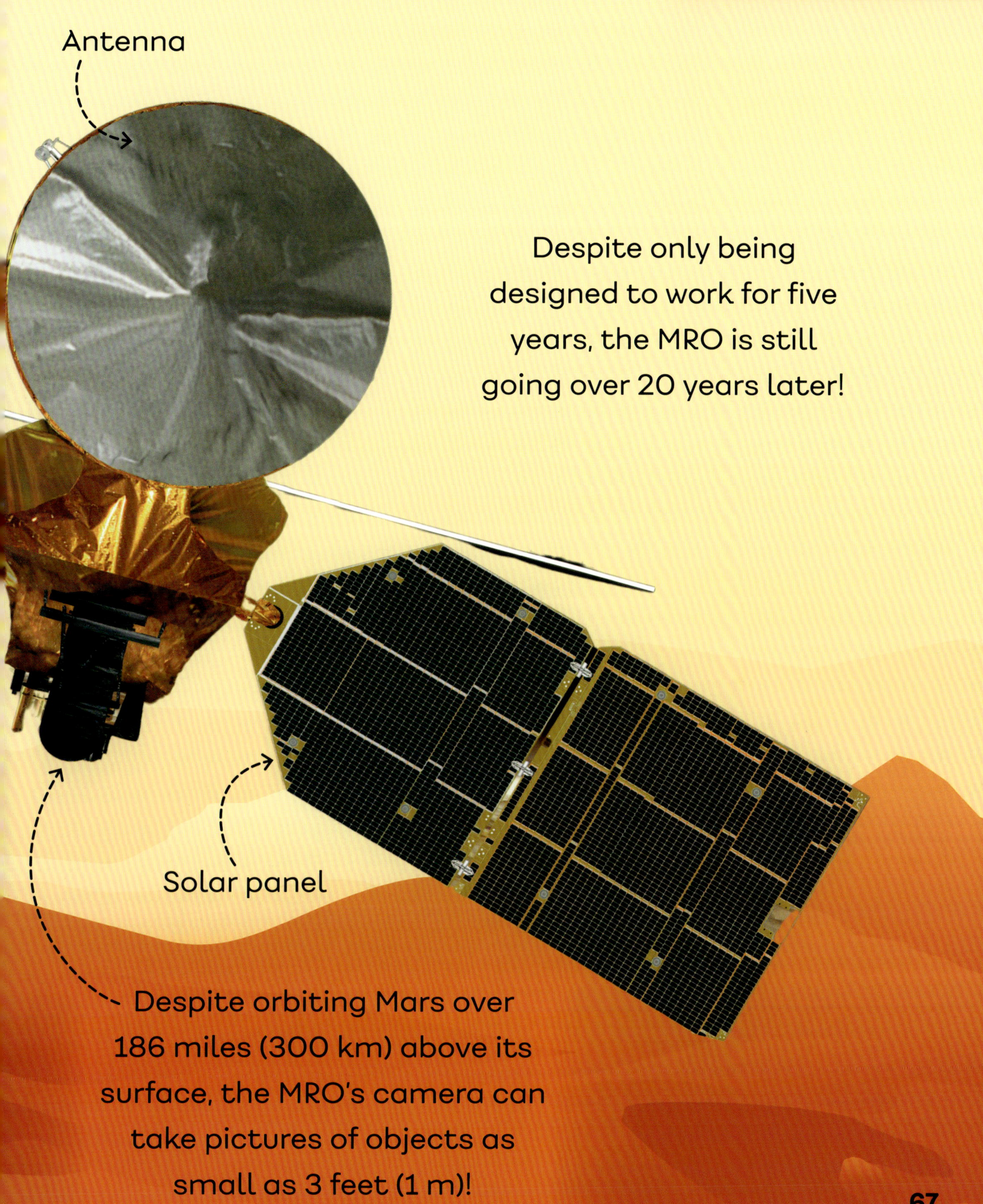

Despite only being designed to work for five years, the MRO is still going over 20 years later!

Despite orbiting Mars over 186 miles (300 km) above its surface, the MRO's camera can take pictures of objects as small as 3 feet (1 m)!

New Horizons

The New Horizons space probe launched in 2006 and flew past Pluto in 2015. It took the first close-up pictures of the **dwarf planet** and is now exploring the farthest parts of our solar system.

New Horizons travels 300 million miles per year!

The long-range camera, LORRI, takes pictures of objects that are very far away.

One instrument on New Horizons examines the solar wind, tiny charged **particles** that come from the Sun.

New Horizons will keep going even after it leaves our solar system!

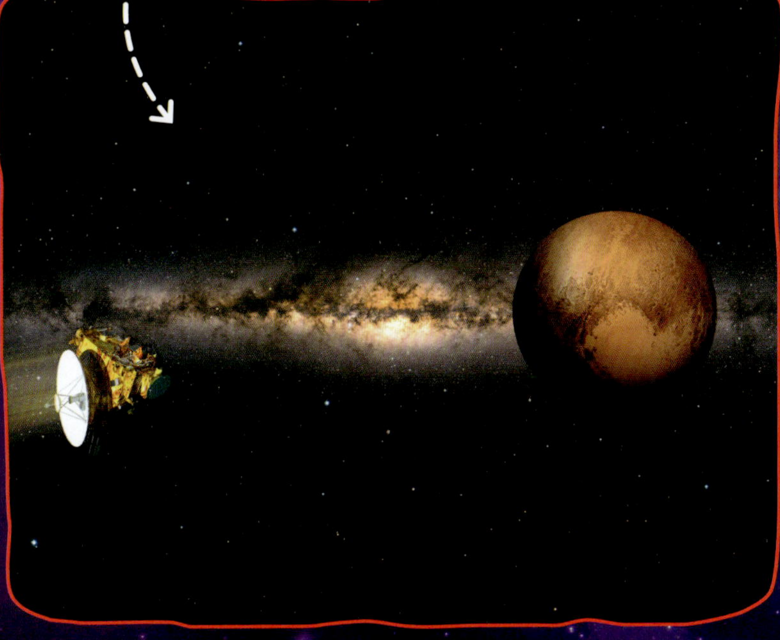

Colorful (colourful) pictures are taken by a camera called Ralph.

Jason-3

Jason-3 is a satellite that studies Earth's oceans. It measures sea levels and other information about the ocean. It was launched in 2016.

Jason-3's altimeter measures how high ocean waves are and how rough the water is.

Another tool, called DORIS, receives radar signals from Earth. It uses them to find out exactly where the satellite is.

Its radiometer is a tool that checks the amount of water in the air.

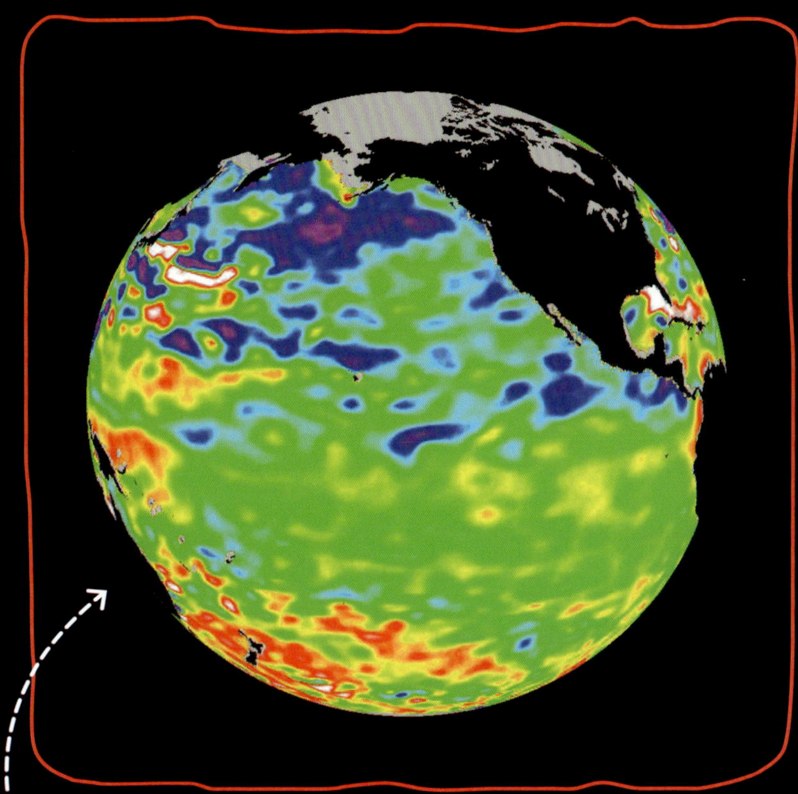

The data collected by Jason-3 helps scientists to understand how ocean water moves and how Earth's climate is changing.

James Webb Space Telescope

The James Webb Space Telescope (JWST) is a powerful telescope that looks deep into space to study stars, galaxies, and planets.

The main mirror is made up of 18 parts, each one covered in gold to help reflect light.

Small trim flaps help to keep the satellite stable.

JWST orbits the Sun at about 1 million miles (1.6 million km) farther out than the Earth does.

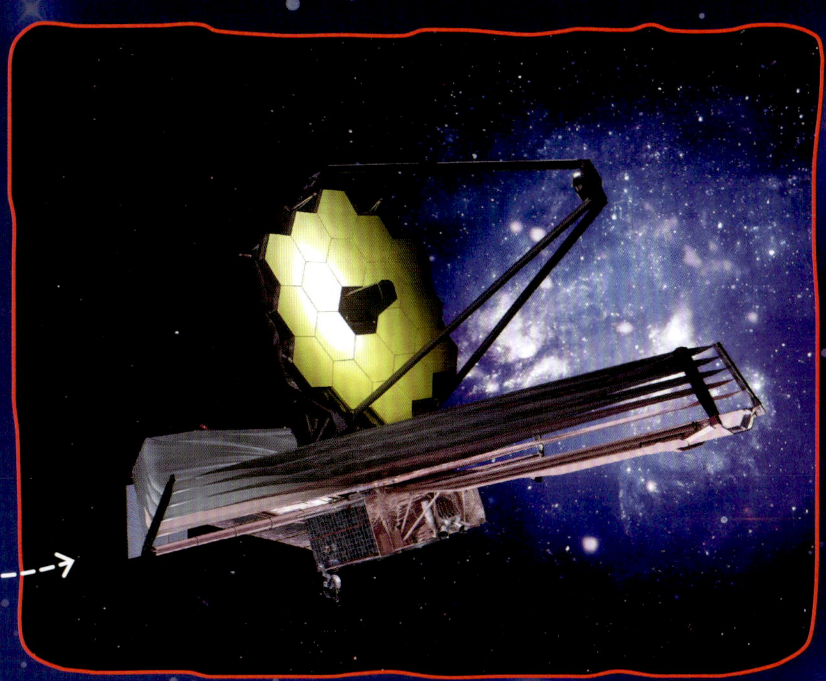

A smaller mirror focuses light from the main mirror so the telescope "sees" better.

A five-layer shield protects the telescope from light and heat.

CubeSat

Not all satellites are big! CubeSats are tiny satellites, often the size of a shoebox. But they still teach scientists a lot!

Because they are so small, many CubeSats can be launched together. In 2021, 143 CubeSats were launched on one rocket!

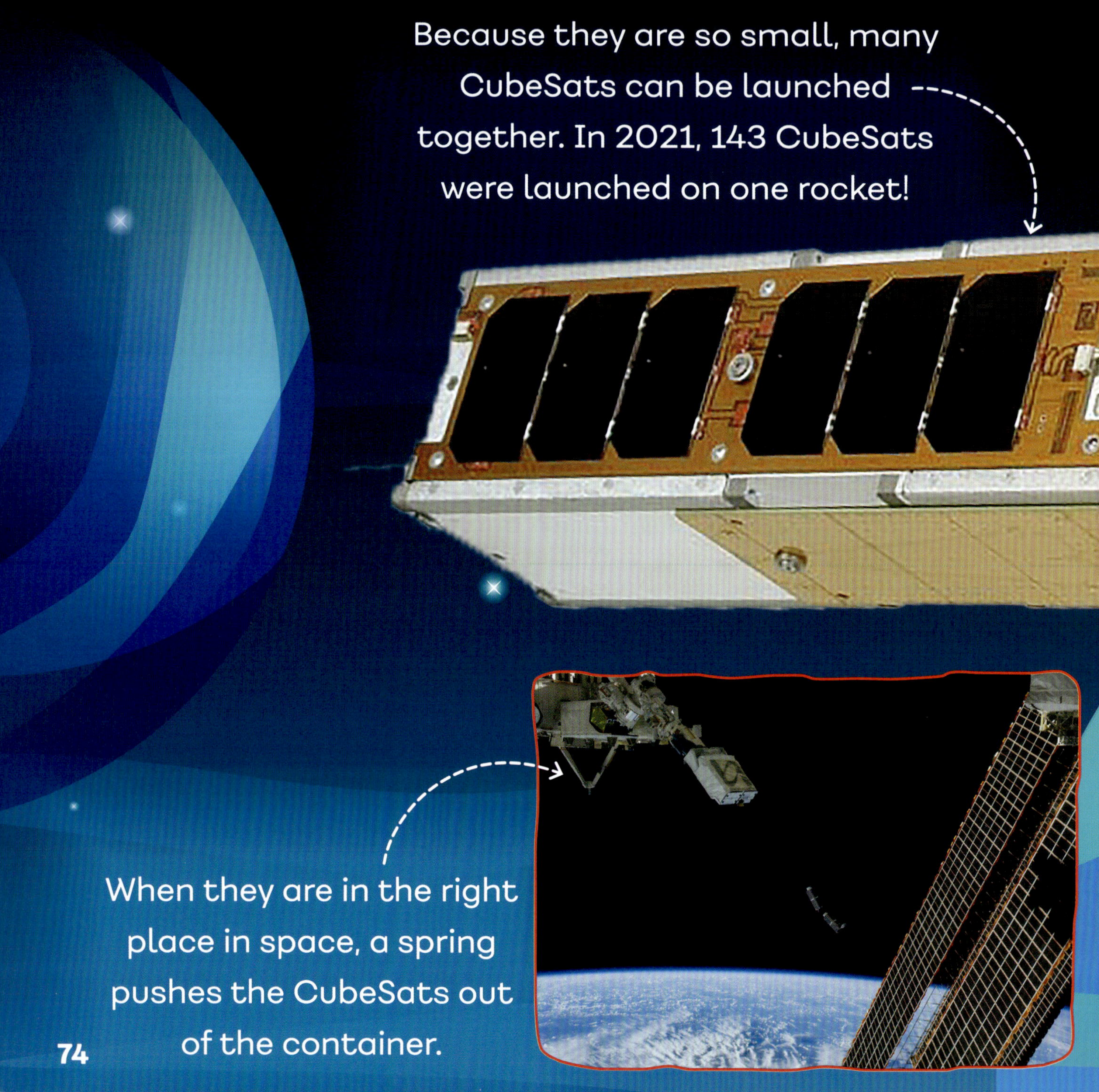

When they are in the right place in space, a spring pushes the CubeSats out of the container.

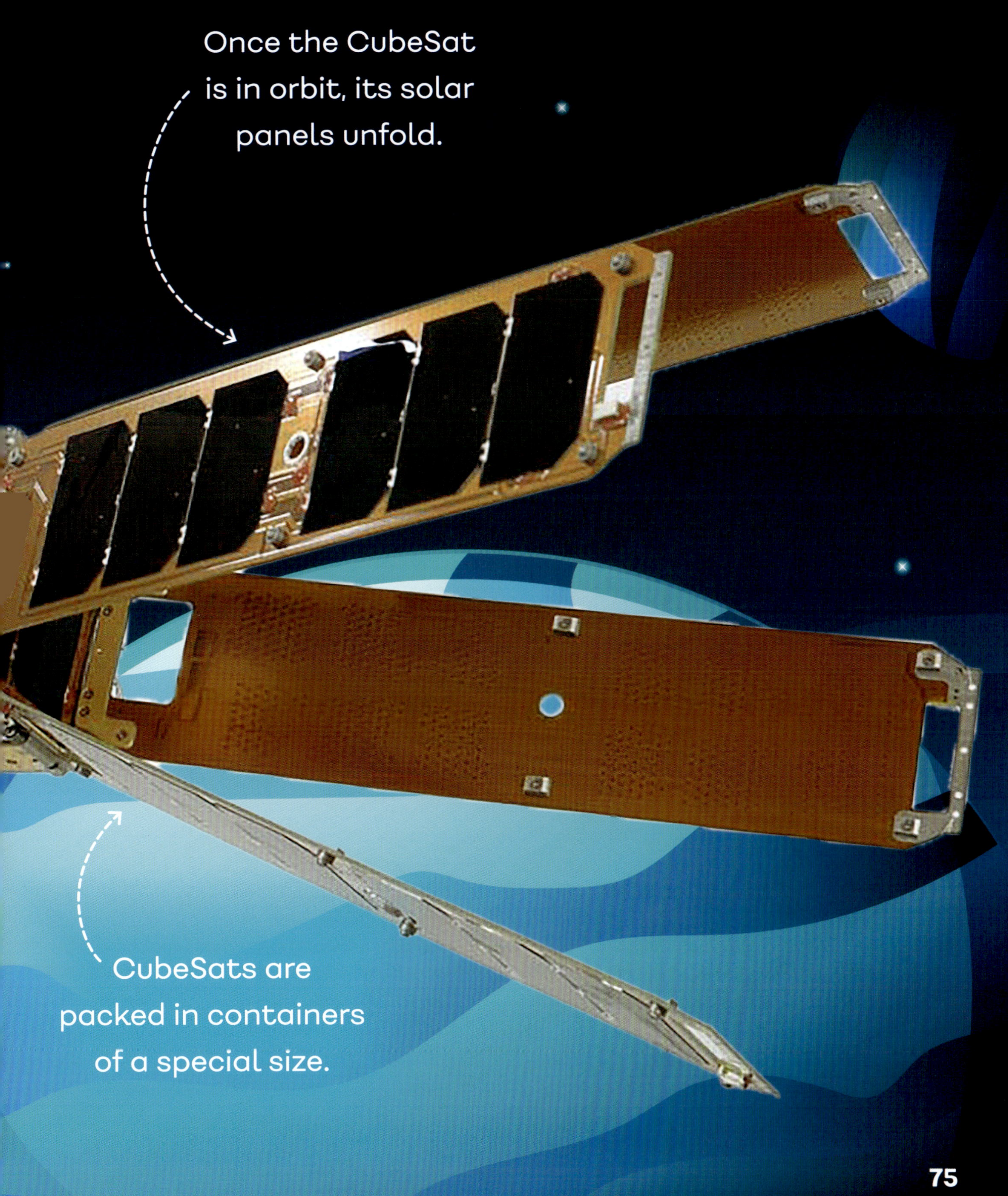

Once the CubeSat is in orbit, its solar panels unfold.

CubeSats are packed in containers of a special size.

Europa Clipper

Launched in 2024, the Europa Clipper spacecraft is flying to Jupiter's moon Europa to study its icy ocean. Scientists think that Europa might have the right conditions for alien life!

When the spacecraft reaches Jupiter in 2030, it will use its engines as brakes to slow down!

The spacecraft is carrying nine scientific instruments inside a **vault** with thick walls to protect them.

The Europa Clipper spacecraft is about 100 feet (30.5 m) long. That's longer than a basketball court!

A dust analyzer will study the pieces of ice and dust that fly off Europa when it is hit by tiny space rocks.

Glossary

Ancient – from a very long time ago.

Asteroid – a small, rocky object that flies around the Sun, especially between Mars' and Jupiter's orbits.

Astronaut - a person trained to travel into outer space.

Bays – separate parts within a piece of equipment where you can keep things.

Bulky – difficult to move or carry because of being large.

Carbon – a material found in all living things and things like coal, diamonds, and pencil lead.

Cargo – goods carried by a large vehicle.

Command module – the part of the Apollo spacecraft that astronauts returned from the Moon in.

Cosmonaut – an astronaut who is from the former Soviet Union (see "Soviet Union").

Crewed – having or being operated by a group of people.

Debris – small pieces of rock, metal, etc. that are left behind after something has broken down or been destroyed.

Docked – connected to another spacecraft or a space station so people or cargo can move between them.

Dwarf planet – large, round objects that orbit the Sun, but aren't big enough to be called planets

Fueling – supplying something with a material that can power it, such as gas (fuel).

Generators – machines that make electricity.

Gravity – the force that pulls objects in space toward each other. On Earth, gravity pulls things down (toward the middle of the planet).

Hatch – the door of a spacecraft.

Instruments – tools or devices that are used for a specific task, like scientific work.

Modified – changed in some way on purpose.

Navigation – finding and following a path to get to a place.

Obstacles – things that block someone or something's way.

Orbit – the path an object takes as it travels around a star, planet, etc.

Orbited – moved in a curved path around a star, planet, etc.

Oxygen – a gas in the air that people and other living things need to breathe.

Particles – tiny pieces of something.

Payload – the people and things being carried for the purpose of a space flight.

Radar – a system that uses radio waves to find the location of objects or to find out the distance, speed, or direction of objects.

Soviet Union – a large country made up of Russia and nearby countries that were ruled as one country from 1922 to 1991.

Stabilizers – things that prevent changes or movements and keep something steady.

Technician – a person who works on or looks after equipment.

Telescopes – instruments that are used make faraway objects in space appear bigger, making them easier to study.

Trenches – long, narrow, and deep holes in the ground.

Vault – a room or storage area with thick walls to keep the things inside it safe.

Index